Good Housekeeping

pasta

HEARST BOOKS

A division of Sterling Publishing Co., Inc.

New York / London

www.sterlingpublishing.com

The Good Housekeeping Triple-Test Promise

We make sure that every recipe that bears the **Good Housekeeping** name works in any oven, with any brand of ingredient, no matter what. That's why, in our test kitchens at the **Good Housekeeping Research Institute,** we test each recipe at least three times—and, often, several more times after that.

When a recipe is first developed one member of our team prepares the dish and we judge it on these criteria: It must be **delicious, family-friendly, healthy,** and **easy to make.**

1. The recipe is then tested several times to fine-tune the flavor and ease of preparation, always by the same team member, using the same equipment.

2. Next, another team member follows the recipe as written, **varying the brands of ingredients and kinds of equipment.** Even the types of stoves we use are changed.

3. A third team member repeats the whole process **using yet another set of equipment and alternative ingredients.**

By the time our recipes appear on these pages, they are guaranteed to work in any kitchen, including yours. WE PROMISE.

Contents

Foreword

Welcome to *Good Housekeeping*'s collection of favorite pasta recipes. With this new 100 Best series, we've gathered the tried-and-true recipes that our editors and readers tell us they make again and again.

If, like many cooks, you rely on pasta a few nights a week, you'll find dozens of recipes that can be prepared while the pasta water boils. Whether you're shopping the express lane of the grocery store or finding inspiration at your local farmer's market, there are recipes to suit.

If you like to keep dinner in the freezer, whip up our Big-Batch Tomato Sauce—you can stir in everything from store-bought meatballs to fresh shrimp or clams and deliver dinner in a flash. Having a crowd over? No problem. Check out our baked pasta chapter where you'll find Sunday Baked Ziti and Meatball Casserole, Spaghetti Carbonara Pie, Butternut-Squash Lasagna, and more great crowd pleasers. Better yet, many of our baked pasta dishes can be prepared ahead, so all you have to do is heat them up when the guests arrive.

Another pasta plus is versatility. You can turn pasta into a wonderfully hearty soup, like our Sausage Pasta Fagioli with Spinach, or toss it with greens and tuna to make a sublime Provençal Pasta Salad—perfect for a picnic supper or light dinner. Combined with cheese, pasta makes a delicious, protein-rich meatless meal. Even meat eaters will love our Swiss Chard Lasagna, with its layers of creamy Parmesan sauce.

And of course, you can dress pasta up or down. For special occasions you'll find an array of impressive dishes to choose from, like our luscious Seafood-Stuffed Shells and Mafalda with Veal and Rosemary. For everyday family meals we offer our creamiest ever Macaroni and Cheese DeLuxe, Linguine with Broccoli and Clams, and Spaghetti and Meatballs plus lots of quick and easy stove-top pastas starring fresh seasonal vegetables.

Each and every one of the recipes has been *triple* tested in the *Good Housekeeping* kitchen to ensure superb results every time you make it. Many of the recipes are classic Italian, while others are inspired by the cuisines of China, Vietnam, Greece, and France. Just be assured that from pasta soups to salads, light side dishes to hearty baked pasta, one common thread runs throughout all 100 of our very best pasta recipes—great taste.

Susan Westmoreland
FOOD DIRECTOR, GOOD HOUSEKEEPING

Great Pasta, Every Time

Perfectly cooked pasta is firm yet tender to the bite, or *al dente* as Italians say, with sauce coating each delicious mouthful. Some of the most common mistakes—mushy spaghetti, watery lasagna, sauce that pools in the bottom of the bowl instead of clinging to the noodle—can easily be avoided by following a few simple guidelines.

For best taste and texture, look for pasta, either Italian or American, made from durum wheat flour or semolina flour. Choose pasta packaged in cardboard boxes. The cardboard keeps out light, which can destroy riboflavin, an important nutrient found in pasta. Resist the urge to transfer pasta from the box to a clear decorative container—the original box offers better protection.

Store dried pasta in a cool, dark place for up to a year. Whole-wheat pasta has a shorter shelf life: no longer than six months and sometimes less. Read package instructions to be sure. Fresh pasta should be refrigerated according to package directions, usually for up to a week. It can also be frozen for up to a month. It's best NOT to thaw frozen pasta before cooking.

Use plenty of boiling water. A good rule of thumb is 4 quarts for each pound of pasta. Bring it to a rolling boil (covering the pot hastens the process), then add about 2 teaspoons of salt per pound of pasta. Salted water takes longer to boil, so add the salt just before adding the pasta. Don't be tempted to omit the salt, it's essential for proper seasoning.

Stir frequently to prevent sticking. Once you've salted the water and it's at a full boil, stir in the pasta. Cover the pot, if necessary, to return water quickly to a boil. Uncover and continue cooking, stirring often until the strands separate. There's no need to add oil to pasta cooking water. In fact, the oil might keep the sauce from adhering to the pasta. Stirring is all you need to prevent sticking.

Cook according to package directions. There's no set rule for how long each pasta shape should cook. Spaghetti from one manufacturer may take longer than the same size spaghetti from another, depending on the type of wheat used and how it was processed. So always read the box— it will give you the correct cooking time.

Check for doneness often before the suggested cooking time has elapsed. The goal is pasta that's tender yet still slightly firm or *al dente*.

The only way to test it is by tasting. Remove a piece from the pot and rinse it briefly under warm water, then taste. There should be no hard white center. Remember that the pasta will continue cooking from the residual heat even after draining. If the cooked pasta will be baked later, undercook it slightly.

Drain well in a colander, shaking to make sure all excess water has been removed. Don't rinse pasta unless the recipe specifies to do so. Rinsing can remove starch that helps the sauce cling and provides important nutrients.

The Shape of Pastas to Come

The recipes in this book use a wide variety of Italian pastas and Asian noodles, ranging from the familiar macaroni and spaghetti to the more exotic *creste di gallo* and rice noodles. In most cases, particularly if a shape is not common, the ingredients list will suggest an easily found substitution. If you don't recognize the particular pasta called for in a recipe, this glossary tells you what to look for.

LONG STRANDS

Capellini: Sometimes called "angel hair." Very thin spaghetti.
Fusilli: Long, wavy strands, "corkscrew pasta."
Spaghetti: Long, thin round strands.
Vermicelli: Very thin spaghetti.

FLAT RIBBONS

Egg noodles: Short, flat, and slightly curled when dry. No-yolk versions are widely available.
Fettuccine: Flat noodles, ¼ inch wide.
Lasagna: Wide, flat pasta. Available in "no-cook" form.
Linguine: Thin pasta ribbons, ⅛ inch wide.
Mafalda: Wide ribbons with a ruffled edge.
Tagliatelle: A little wider than fettuccine.

TUBULAR PASTAS

Elbow macaroni: Small curved tubular pasta.
Penne: Pasta tubes with diagonal ends.
Rigatoni: Large ribbed tubes.
Ziti: Medium tubes.

SMALL PASTAS

Campanelle: Tiny bell-shaped pasta.
Cavatappi: Small corkscrews.
Ditalini: Short tubular pasta; also called tubettini.
Orechini: Pasta "earrings."
Orzo: Rice-shaped pasta.

ONE-OF-A-KIND PASTAS

Cavatelli: Short ridged pasta.
Conchiglie: Medium shells.
Creste di gallo: Curved pasta with ridged edge.
Farfalle: Literal translation is "butterflies"; known in America as bow ties.
Gemelli: Two short strands of pasta that have been twisted together.

Pasta e Piselli

This light take on *pasta e fagiole* (the classic bean and pasta soup) makes a soothing weeknight meal. If they're in season, use fresh peas (*piselli*). Cook them in the broth until tender before adding the pasta.

PREP 10 minutes plus cooking pasta   COOK 20 minutes
MAKES about 10 cups or 5 main-dish servings

2 tablespoons olive oil

3 garlic cloves, crushed with side of chef's knife

1 can (14½ ounces) diced tomatoes

2 cans (14½ ounces each) chicken broth or 3½ cups Chicken Broth (page 16)

½ cup water

¼ cup loosely packed fresh basil leaves, coarsely chopped

8 ounces mixed pasta, such as penne, bow ties, or elbow macaroni (2 cups), cooked as label directs

1 package (10 ounces) frozen peas, thawed

freshly grated Parmesan cheese

1. In nonreactive 4-quart saucepan, heat oil over medium heat. Add garlic; cook, stirring frequently, until golden, about 2 minutes.

2. Add tomatoes with their juice, broth, water, and basil; heat to boiling. Reduce heat; cover and simmer 5 minutes. Discard garlic.

3. Stir in pasta and peas; heat through. Serve with Parmesan.

EACH SERVING WITHOUT PARMESAN About 317 calories |
12 g protein | 51 g carbohydrate | 8 g total fat (1 g saturated) |
0 mg cholesterol | 1,044 mg sodium.

Trattoria-Style Pasta and Beans

A sprinkling of fresh parsley and Parmesan cheese provides the perfect finishing touch for this comforting Italian meal-in-a-bowl.

⏱ **PREP** 15 minutes **COOK** 40 minutes
MAKES about 8 cups or 4 main-dish servings

1 cup tubetti or ditalini pasta

1 tablespoon olive oil

1 medium onion, finely chopped

1 carrot, finely chopped

1 celery stalk, finely chopped

1 garlic clove, minced

1 can (15½ to 19 ounces) no-salt-added white kidney beans (cannellini), rinsed and drained

1 can (14½ ounces) diced tomatoes

½ teaspoon salt

¼ teaspoon coarsely ground black pepper

4 cups water

¼ cup grated Parmesan cheese

¼ cup loosely packed fresh parsley leaves, chopped

1. In 3-quart saucepan, cook pasta as label directs.

2. Meanwhile, in 4-quart saucepan, heat oil over medium heat until hot. Add onion, carrot, and celery, and cook 15 minutes or until vegetables are tender, stirring occasionally. Add garlic and cook 1 minute, stirring.

3. Add beans, tomatoes, salt, pepper, and water; heat to boiling over high heat. Reduce heat to medium-low and simmer, uncovered, 20 minutes.

4. Drain pasta. Into mixture in saucepan, stir pasta, Parmesan, and parsley; heat through.

EACH SERVING About 295 calories | 14 g protein | 48 g carbohydrate | 6 g total fat (2 g saturated) | 4 mg cholesterol | 865 mg sodium.

Tortellini in Brodo

This stick to your ribs soup is perfect for a cold winter's day. If you're short on time, you can use canned broth, but homemade will taste even better.

PREP 5 minutes   COOK 15 minutes   MAKES 4 first-course or 2 main-dish servings

8 ounces cheese or meat tortellini

5 cups chicken broth (recipe below)

1 carrot, cut into small dice

$^1/_2$ teaspoon salt

$^1/_2$ cup grated Parmesan cheese

$^1/_4$ cup chopped fresh basil

1. In a large saucepot, cook the pasta according to package directions; drain.

2. Meanwhile, in a medium saucepan, bring the broth to a boil over high heat. Add the carrot and salt and cook until the carrot is tender, about 3 minutes. Add the cooked tortellini; reduce to a simmer and cook 1 minute.

3. Place 2 tablespoons of Parmesan and 1 tablespoon of basil in each of 4 soup bowls. Ladle the broth, carrot, and tortellini into the bowls and serve.

HOMEMADE CHICKEN BROTH In 6-quart saucepot, combine **1 chicken (3 to 3½ pounds), including neck** (reserve giblets for another use), **2 carrots,** peeled and cut into 2-inch pieces, **1 stalk celery**, cut into 2-inch pieces, **1 medium onion,** cut into quarters, **5 parsley sprigs**, **1 garlic clove**, ½ **teaspoon dried thyme**, **1 bay leaf,** and **3 quarts water** or enough to cover; heat to boiling over high heat. Skim foam from surface. Reduce heat and simmer 1 hour, turning chicken once and skimming. Remove from heat; transfer chicken to large bowl. When cool enough to handle, remove skin and bones from chicken. (Reserve the chicken for another use.) Return skin and bones to Dutch oven and heat to boiling. Skim foam; reduce heat and simmer 3 hours. Strain the broth through colander into large bowl; discard solids. Strain again through sieve into containers; cool. Cover and refrigerate to use within 3 days, or freeze up to 4 months. To use, skim and discard fat from surface of broth. Makes 5 cups.

EACH FIRST-COURSE SERVING About 180 calories | 13 g protein | 20 g carbohydrate | 6 g total fat (3 g saturated) | 17 mg cholesterol | 735 mg sodium.

Vietnamese Noodle Soup

Basil and cilantro, staples of southeast Asian cuisines, give this light soup sparkling flavor. Look for rice noodles in Asian markets. If you can't find them, ramen noodles (without the flavor packet) make a good substitute.

PREP 20 minutes **COOK** 20 minutes
MAKES about 8 cups or 4 main-dish servings

1 large lime	2 cups water
4 ounces dried flat rice noodles (about ¼ inch wide)	4 ounces shiitake mushrooms, stems discarded and caps thinly sliced
2 cans (14½ ounces each) chicken broth or vegetable broth	4 ounces snow peas, strings removed and each pod cut diagonally in half
1 small bunch fresh basil	
2 garlic cloves, crushed with side of chef's knife	1 tablespoon soy sauce
1 piece (2 inches) peeled fresh ginger, thinly sliced	1 cup loosely packed fresh cilantro leaves, chopped

1. From lime, with vegetable peeler, remove peel and reserve; squeeze 1 tablespoon juice.

2. In large bowl, pour enough *boiling water* over rice noodles to cover; let soak 7 to 10 minutes to soften.

3. Meanwhile, in 3-quart saucepan, place broth, basil, garlic, ginger, lime peel, and water; heat to boiling over high heat. Reduce heat to low; cover and simmer 10 minutes. Strain broth through sieve; discard solids and return broth to saucepan.

4. Drain noodles; rinse under cold running water and drain again. Stir mushrooms, snow peas, soy sauce, and noodles into broth mixture; heat to boiling over high heat. Reduce heat to low; cover and simmer for 3 minutes. Stir in cilantro and lime juice just before serving.

EACH SERVING About 155 calories | 5 g protein | 30 g carbohydrate |
2 g total fat (1 g saturated) | 0 mg cholesterol | 1,120 mg sodium.

Pasta and Pepper Toss with Summer Basil

This colorful mix of sweet yellow and red peppers, tomatoes, eggplant, and zucchini can be served hot or at room temperature. It's a natural for picnics and potlucks.

PREP 45 minutes   **COOK** 35 minutes   **MAKES** 12 accompaniment servings

3 medium red peppers

2 medium yellow peppers

1 package (16 ounces) penne, radiatore, or fusilli pasta

4 tablespoons olive oil

1 medium red onion, chopped

3 medium zucchini (6 ounces each), each cut lengthwise in half then thinly sliced crosswise

1 medium eggplant (1¼ pounds), cut into ½-inch chunks

¾ teaspoon salt

3 ripe medium tomatoes (1 pound), chopped

1 cup loosely packed fresh basil leaves, chopped

2 tablespoons capers, drained

1. Preheat broiler. Line broiling pan (without rack) with foil. Cut each pepper lengthwise in half; discard stems and seeds. With hand, flatten each pepper half. Place peppers (half the amount at a time, if broiling pan is small), cut side down, in broiling pan. Place pan in broiler 5 to 6 inches from source of heat and broil peppers until charred and blistered, 10 to 15 minutes. Wrap foil around peppers and allow to steam at room temperature 15 minutes or until cool enough to handle. (Repeat with remaining peppers.)

2. Meanwhile in large saucepot, cook pasta as label directs; drain. Rinse with cold water, and drain again. Set aside.

3. Remove peppers from foil. Peel off skin and discard. Cut peppers into ½-inch pieces.

4. In nonstick 12-inch skillet, heat 1 tablespoon oil over medium heat until hot. Add onion and cook 6 minutes or until tender, stirring occasionally. Add zucchini and 1 tablespoon oil, and cook 7 minutes or until zucchini are tender-crisp, stirring frequently. Add eggplant, salt, and remaining 2 tablespoons oil, and cook 8 minutes or until eggplant is tender, stirring frequently.

5. Transfer vegetables to large bowl; stir in tomatoes, basil, capers, and ½ teaspoon salt. Add pasta; toss well. Serve salad warm, or cover and refrigerate until ready to serve.

EACH SERVING About 225 calories | 7 g protein | 38 g carbohydrate | 6 g total fat (1 g saturated) | 0 mg cholesterol | 285 mg sodium.

GH Test Kitchen Tip

Use any short pasta and substitute yellow summer squash for all or part of the zucchini.

Pasta Salad with Lemon and Peas

This super simple salad makes a nice change from potato salad at picnics. Try it with anything from chicken to grilled steak.

PREP 20 minutes   **COOK** 20 minutes
MAKES about 10 cups or 12 accompaniment servings

1 pound bow-tie or small shell pasta	1 teaspoon salt
1 package (10 ounces) frozen baby peas	$\frac{1}{4}$ teaspoon coarsely ground black pepper
2 lemons	1 cup loosely packed fresh basil leaves, chopped
$\frac{2}{3}$ cup milk	4 green onions, thinly sliced
$\frac{1}{2}$ cup light mayonnaise	

1. In large saucepot, cook pasta as label directs, adding frozen peas during last 2 minutes of cooking time. Drain pasta and peas; rinse with cold water and drain well.

2. Meanwhile, from lemons, grate 1 tablespoon peel and squeeze 3 tablespoons juice. In large bowl, with wire whisk, mix lemon peel and juice with milk, mayonnaise, salt, pepper, basil, and green onions until blended.

3. Add pasta and peas to mayonnaise dressing; toss to coat well. Cover and refrigerate up to two days if not serving right away.

EACH SERVING About 207 calories | 7 g protein | 33 g carbohydrate | 4 g total fat (1 g saturated) | 5 mg cholesterol | 327 mg sodium.

Provençal Pasta Salad

The signature flavors of southern France—garlic, tomatoes, peppers, and olive oil—are featured in this robust salad. For an authentic finishing touch, drizzle with a little extravirgin olive oil before serving.

🍲 **PREP** 30 minutes **COOK** 30 minutes
MAKES about 12 cups or 6 main-dish servings

1 package (16 ounces) bow-tie pasta	¾ teaspoon salt
2 medium red peppers or 1 jar (7 ounces) roasted red peppers, drained and cut into ½-inch pieces	¼ teaspoon coarsely ground black pepper
2 tablespoons olive oil	1 pint cherry tomatoes, each cut in half
1 medium onion, chopped	1 cup loosely packed fresh basil leaves, coarsely chopped
1 small eggplant (about ¾ pound), cut into ½-inch chunks	⅓ cup kalamata olives, pitted and coarsely chopped
2 garlic cloves, minced	

1. In large saucepot, cook pasta as label directs. Reserve *¼ cup pasta cooking water*. Drain and rinse pasta under cold running water; drain again.

2. Meanwhile, roast peppers if using fresh ones. Preheat broiler. Line broiling pan (without rack) with foil. Cut each pepper lengthwise in half; discard stems and seeds. Place peppers, cut side down, in broiling pan. With hand, flatten each pepper half. Place pan in broiler 5 to 6 inches from source of heat, and broil peppers until skins are charred and blistered, 10 to 15 minutes. Wrap foil around peppers and allow to steam at room temperature 15 minutes or until cool enough to handle. Remove peppers from foil. Peel off skins and discard. Cut peppers into ½-inch pieces.

3. In nonstick 12-inch skillet, heat oil over medium heat until hot. Add onion and cook about 10 minutes or until tender and golden, stirring often. Increase heat to medium-high. Add the eggplant, garlic, salt, and black pepper and cook 8 minutes longer or until the eggplant is tender and golden, stirring often.

4. To pasta, add roasted peppers, onion mixture, tomatoes, basil, olives, and reserved pasta cooking water; toss gently. Transfer pasta mixture to serving bowl. Cover and refrigerate if not serving right away.

EACH SERVING About 373 calories | 11 g protein | 67 g carbohydrate | 7 g total fat (1 g saturated) | 0 mg cholesterol | 460 mg sodium.

Ricotta Gnocchi with Brown Butter and Fresh Herbs

There's no need to be intimidated—these gnocchi are a snap to make. A simple butter and herb sauce is the only dressing up they need.

⊘ PREP I hour   COOK 17 minutes   MAKES 8 first-course servings

3 tablespoons butter

I teaspoon chopped fresh sage

¾ teaspoon salt

¼ teaspoon ground black pepper

I container (15 ounces) ricotta cheese

6 tablespoons freshly grated Parmesan cheese

¾ cup chopped fresh parsley

¾ cup all-purpose flour or as needed

1. In 2-quart saucepan, melt butter over medium heat. Continue to cook, stirring, until butter turns golden brown. (If butter gets too dark, it will be bitter.) Remove from heat and add sage, ¼ teaspoon salt, and pepper; set aside.

2. In medium bowl, combine ricotta, Parmesan, parsley, and remaining ½ teaspoon salt. Sprinkle flour over ricotta mixture and, with your hands, work mixture into soft, smooth dough. If dough is sticky, add some flour. Work dough just until flour is incorporated into cheese mixture; do not overwork.

3. Break off piece of dough; on a lightly floured surface, roll into ¾-inch-thick rope. (If rope doesn't hold together, return to bowl with remaining dough and work in more flour.) Cut dough rope into ¾-inch lengths. Place one piece of dough on inside curve of fork tines, gently pressing on dough with thumb as you roll dough along tines. Allow dough to drop off fork, slightly curling in on itself, forming an oval. One side of gnocchi will have ridges and opposite side will have an indentation. Repeat rolling, cutting, and shaping with remaining dough. (Gnocchi can be made up to 4 hours ahead to this point. Arrange in floured jelly-roll pan; cover and refrigerate.)

4. In 5-quart saucepot, heat *4 quarts water* to boiling over high heat. Add half of gnocchi and cook until gnocchi float to surface, 2 to 3 minutes. With slotted spoon, transfer gnocchi to warm shallow serving bowl. Repeat with remaining gnocchi. To serve, toss gnocchi with sage butter.

EACH SERVING About 196 calories | 9 g protein | 11 g carbohydrate | 13 g total fat (8 g saturated) | 42 mg cholesterol | 394 mg sodium.

Butternut-Squash Gnocchi with Sage

In Italy's Friuli region, gnocchi are made with butternut squash instead of just potato, flour, or farina. Lidia Bastianich, the renowned Italian chef and restaurant owner, gave us this luscious recipe. She says the gnocchi will be lighter if the potatoes are mashed when hot (see photo on page 9).

PREP 1 hour plus cooling   COOK 30 minutes   MAKES 6 accompaniment servings

GNOCCHI

1 small butternut squash
   (1½ pounds), cut lengthwise
   in half, peeled, seeded, and
   cut into 2-inch chunks

2 medium baking potatoes
   (8 ounces each), peeled and
   cut into 2-inch chunks

2 large eggs

½ cup grated Parmesan cheese

1¼ teaspoons salt

pinch ground nutmeg

1 to 1¼ cups all-purpose flour plus
   additional for dusting

SAGE SAUCE

1½ cups reduced-sodium chicken
   broth

½ cup butter (1 stick)

12 fresh sage leaves

½ cup grated Parmesan cheese

4 ounces coarsely grated ricotta
   salata or Parmesan cheese
   (optional)

coarsely ground black pepper for
   garnish

1. Prepare the gnocchi: Place the squash in microwave-safe baking dish; cover and cook in microwave on High 9 to 11 minutes, until the squash is tender when pierced with tip of a knife.

2. Place squash chunks in food mill fitted with fine disk and press into medium bowl (or press through medium-mesh sieve). Place 4 layers paper towels on work surface; spoon squash puree onto paper towels. Cover squash with 4 more layers paper towel; press lightly with hands to remove excess moisture from squash. Repeat process with dry paper towels 3 more times or until squash is reduced to about ¾ cup.

3. Meanwhile, place potato chunks in microwave-safe baking dish with *2 tablespoons water*. Cover baking dish and cook potatoes in microwave on High 9 to 11 minutes, until potato is tender when pierced with tip of knife.

4. Place potato chunks in food mill fitted with fine disk and press into medium bowl (or mash in bowl with potato masher). Spread warm mashed potatoes in thin, even layer in 15½" by 10½" jelly-roll pan, without pressing or compacting; cool. Line another jelly-roll pan with kitchen towel; lightly dust with flour and set aside.

5. In large bowl, with wire whisk, lightly beat eggs. Beat in squash, potato, Parmesan, salt, and nutmeg until blended. With spoon, stir in ¾ cup flour just until combined. Turn dough onto lightly floured surface and knead in another ¼ to ½ cup flour, just until a soft dough forms. (Do not overknead dough or the gnocchi will be heavy and tough.) Divide the dough into 4 equal pieces.

6. With floured hands, roll 1 piece dough into ½-inch-thick rope. Slice rope into ½-inch pieces. Hold fork on work surface; with floured thumb, roll 1 dough piece lightly on fork toward tip of tines. As dough wraps around tip of thumb, it will form a dumpling with a deep indentation on 1 side and a ridged surface on the other. Place gnocchi in towel-lined pan.

7. Repeat Step 6 with remaining dough. (At this point gnocchi must be cooked immediately or frozen. To freeze gnocchi, place in a single layer on cookie sheet; freeze until very firm. Transfer to freezer-weight self-sealing plastic bag.)

8. Fill 6-quart saucepot half full of *water*; add 1 teaspoon salt if desired. Over high heat, heat to boiling. Add one-fourth gnocchi to boiling water, stirring gently with wooden spoon. After all gnocchi rise to surface, cook 3 to 5 minutes longer, until cooked through. With slotted spoon, remove gnocchi to paper towels to drain. Repeat with remaining gnocchi.

9. Prepare sage sauce: In 12-inch skillet, heat chicken broth, butter, and sage to boiling over high heat. Boil 2 minutes.

10. Add cooked gnocchi to sauce in skillet; reduce heat to medium. Cook gnocchi 5 minutes or until heated through, stirring gently with wooden spoon or heat-safe rubber spatula. Stir in ½ cup grated Parmesan.

11. Spoon gnocchi with sauce into 6 bowls; sprinkle with ricotta salata, and black pepper.

EACH SERVING WITHOUT RICOTTA SALATA **About 425 calories** |
13 g protein | **43 g carbohydrate** | **23 g total fat (14 g saturated)** |
126 mg cholesterol | **1,040 mg sodium.**

Spaghetti with Oil and Garlic Sauce

Cooking mellows the garlic, creating a light yet flavorful sauce. If you like, toss in some chopped and pitted Kalamata olives or chopped dried tomatoes. Serve with freshly grated Parmesan cheese.

PREP 5 minutes **COOK** 25 minutes **MAKES** 6 main-dish servings

1 package (16 ounces) spaghetti or linguine

$\frac{1}{4}$ cup olive oil

1 large garlic clove, finely chopped

$\frac{1}{8}$ teaspoon crushed red pepper (optional)

$\frac{3}{4}$ teaspoon salt

$\frac{1}{4}$ teaspoon coarsely ground black pepper

2 tablespoons chopped fresh parsley

1. In large saucepot, cook pasta as label directs. Drain.

2. Meanwhile, in 1-quart saucepan, heat oil over medium heat. Add garlic and cook just until golden, about 1 minute; add crushed red pepper, if using, and cook 30 seconds longer. Remove saucepan from heat; stir in salt and black pepper. In warm serving bowl, toss pasta with sauce and parsley.

EACH SERVING About 362 calories | 10 g protein | 57 g carbohydrate | 10 g total fat (1 g saturated) | 0 mg cholesterol | 361 mg sodium.

Marinara Sauce

We use this versatile herbed tomato sauce in several recipes throughout this book, but it's also delicious on its own. For a super quick meal, serve it over cheese ravioli from the refrigerator case.

PREP 5 minutes **COOK** 30 minutes **MAKES** 3½ cups

2 tablespoons olive oil

I small onion, chopped

I garlic clove, finely chopped

I can (28 ounces) plum tomatoes

2 tablespoons tomato paste

2 tablespoons chopped fresh basil or parsley (optional)

½ teaspoon salt

1. In nonreactive 3-quart saucepan, heat oil over medium heat; add onion and garlic and cook, stirring, until onion is tender, about 5 minutes.

2. Stir in tomatoes with their juice, tomato paste, basil, if using, and salt. Heat to boiling, breaking up tomatoes with side of spoon. Reduce heat; partially cover and simmer, stirring occasionally, until sauce has thickened slightly, about 20 minutes. Use to coat 1 pound pasta for 4 main-dish servings.

EACH ½ **CUP About 67 calories** I **I g protein** I **7 g carbohydrate** I **4 g total fat (I g saturated)** I **0 mg cholesterol** I **388 mg sodium.**

Arrabbiata Sauce

Arrabbiata means "angry" in Italian, and this recipe makes a pot of hot-tempered sauce, spiced with crushed red pepper. For a heartier dish, stir 8 ounces of cooked, crumbled sweet Italian sausage into the sauce and serve over spaghetti or penne.

PREP 5 minutes **COOK** 1 hour **MAKES** about 14 cups

½ cup olive oil

6 garlic cloves, crushed with side of
   chef's knife

5 cans (28 ounces each) plum
   tomatoes

1 tablespoon salt

1 to 1½ teaspoons crushed
   red pepper

1. In nonreactive 8-quart saucepot, heat oil over medium heat. Add garlic and cook, stirring, 2 minutes (do not brown). Stir in tomatoes with their juice, salt, and crushed red pepper; heat to boiling over high heat. Reduce heat; simmer, stirring occasionally and breaking up tomatoes with side of spoon, until sauce has thickened slightly, about 40 minutes.

2. If smooth rather than chunky texture is preferred, press sauce through food mill. Use 2½ cups sauce to coat 1 pound pasta for 4 main-dish servings.

EACH ½ **CUP** About 64 calories | 2 g protein | 6 g carbohydrate | 4 g total fat (0 g saturated) | 0 mg cholesterol | 480 mg sodium.

Big-Batch Tomato Sauce

Perfect for baked ziti and lasagna, this recipe makes 10 cups of mildly seasoned sauce. Heat 2 ½ cups of sauce for each pound of pasta (see photo on page 131).

⏲ **PREP** 15 minutes **COOK** 1 hour **MAKES** about 10 cups

3 tablespoons olive oil

3 carrots, peeled and finely chopped

1 large onion (12 ounces), chopped

2 garlic cloves, finely chopped

3 cans (28 ounces each) plum
   tomatoes in puree

1 bay leaf

¾ teaspoon salt

¼ teaspoon coarsely ground
   black pepper

1. In nonreactive 5-quart Dutch oven, heat oil over medium heat. Add carrots and onion and cook, stirring occasionally, until vegetables are very tender, about 20 minutes. Add garlic; cook, stirring, 2 minutes.

2. Add tomatoes with their puree, bay leaf, salt, and pepper to Dutch oven; heat to boiling over high heat, breaking up tomatoes with side of spoon. Reduce heat; cover and simmer 15 minutes. Remove cover and simmer until sauce has thickened slightly, about 20 minutes longer. Discard bay leaf.

EACH ½ **CUP About 58 calories** | **2 g protein** | **10 g carbohydrate** | **2 g total fat (0 g saturated)** | **0 mg cholesterol** | **280 mg sodium.**

Classic Bolognese Sauce

A staple of the cuisine of Bologna, in northern Italy, this tomato-based meat sauce is enriched with cream and mellowed by long simmering. Serve it over fresh fettuccine or penne, rigatoni, or another tubular pasta that will trap the tiny bits of meat and tomato.

PREP 10 minutes   COOK 1 hour 25 minutes   MAKES 5 cups

2 tablespoons olive oil

1 medium onion, chopped

1 carrot, peeled and finely chopped

1 stalk celery, finely chopped

1½ pounds ground meat for meat loaf (beef, pork, and/or veal) or ground beef chuck

½ cup dry red wine

1 can (28 ounces) plum tomatoes, chopped

2 teaspoons salt

¼ teaspoon ground black pepper

⅛ teaspoon ground nutmeg

¼ cup heavy or whipping cream

1. In nonreactive 5-quart Dutch oven, heat oil over medium heat. Add onion, carrot, and celery and cook, stirring occasionally, until tender, about 10 minutes.

2. Add ground meat and cook, breaking up meat with side of spoon, until no longer pink. Stir in wine and heat to boiling. Stir in tomatoes with their juice, salt, pepper, and nutmeg. Heat to boiling over high heat. Reduce heat and simmer, stirring occasionally, 1 hour.

3. Stir in cream and heat through, stirring constantly. Use 2½ cups of sauce to coat 1 pound pasta for 6 main-dish servings.

EACH CUP About 678 calories | 32 g protein | 68 g carbohydrate | 30 g total fat (11 g saturated) | 104 mg cholesterol | 1,210 mg sodium.

No-Cook Tomato Sauce

**A great way to use up fresh farm-stand tomatoes. Toss all 7 cups with
1 pound hot pasta.**

⊘ **PREP** 15 minutes plus 15 minutes to stand **MAKES** about 7 cups

**2 pounds ripe tomatoes (about
    6 medium), cut into ½-inch pieces**

**½ pound fresh mozzarella cheese,
    cut into ½-inch pieces**

**1 cup packed fresh basil leaves, cut
    into strips**

2 tablespoons olive oil

1 tablespoon red wine vinegar

1 teaspoon salt

**¼ teaspoon coarsely ground
    black pepper**

In medium bowl, combine tomatoes with their juice, mozzarella, basil,
olive oil, vinegar, salt, and pepper, stirring gently to mix well. Allow sauce
to stand at room temperature at least 15 minutes or up to 1 hour to
develop flavor.

EACH CUP About 150 calories | 8 g protein | 8 g carbohydrate |
12 g total fat (4 g saturated) | 26 mg cholesterol | 340 mg sodium.

GH Test Kitchen Tip

**The sauce makes a tasty topping for grilled slices of
country bread.**

Spaghetti with Meatballs

This hearty favorite never goes out of style. We like to use a combination of beef, veal, and pork for the richest flavor, but ground chuck is good too. For a lower-fat meal, substitute the Lean Meatballs (page 39).

PREP 20 minutes COOK 1 hour MAKES 6 main-dish servings

Marinara Sauce (page 29)

1½ pounds ground meat for meat loaf (beef, pork, and/or veal) or ground beef chuck

1 cup fresh bread crumbs (about 2 slices bread)

1 large egg

¼ cup freshly grated Pecorino Romano or Parmesan cheese

¼ cup chopped fresh parsley

1 garlic clove, finely chopped

1 teaspoon salt

¼ teaspoon ground black pepper

2 teaspoons olive oil

1 package (16 ounces) spaghetti

1. Prepare marinara sauce.

2. Meanwhile, prepare meatballs: In large bowl, combine ground meat, bread crumbs, egg, Romano, parsley, garlic, salt, and pepper just until blended but not overmixed. Shape into twelve 2-inch meatballs, handling meat as little as possible.

3. In nonstick 10-inch skillet, heat olive oil over medium heat until hot. Add meatballs and cook, gently turning, until browned and just cooked through, about 20 minutes. Stir sauce into meatballs and heat to boiling, stirring to loosen browned bits from the bottom of the skillet.

4. Meanwhile, in large saucepot, cook pasta as label directs. Drain. In warm serving bowl, gently toss pasta with meatballs and sauce.

EACH SERVING About 692 calories | 34 g protein | 69 g carbohydrate | 30 g total fat (10 g saturated) | 129 mg cholesterol | 1,077 mg sodium.

Lean Meatballs

There are two secret ingredients here—bread, which makes the meatballs tender, and turkey, which cuts the fat. Serve them in a tomato sauce over spaghetti or make a meatball sandwich.

◷ PREP 25 minutes BAKE 15 minutes MAKES 24 meatballs

3 slices firm white bread, diced

⅓ cup water

1 pound lean ground beef

1 pound lean ground turkey

2 large egg whites

⅓ cup grated Pecorino Romano or Parmesan cheese

3 tablespoons grated onion

2 tablespoons minced fresh parsley

1 teaspoon salt

¼ teaspoon coarsely ground black pepper

1 garlic clove, minced

1. Preheat oven to 425°F. Line a 15½" by 10 ½" jelly-roll pan with foil; spray with nonstick cooking spray.

2. In large bowl, combine diced bread and water. With hand, mix until bread is evenly moistened. Add ground beef, ground turkey, egg whites, cheese, onion, parsley, salt, pepper, and garlic. With hand, mix until ingredients are well combined.

3. Shape meat mixture into twenty-four 2-inch meatballs. (For easier shaping, use slightly wet hands.) Place meatballs in jelly-roll pan and bake 15 to 20 minutes, until cooked through and lightly browned.

EACH MEATBALL About 70 calories | 9 g protein | 2 g carbohydrate | 3 g total fat (1 g saturated) | 24 mg cholesterol | 140 mg sodium.

GH Test Kitchen Tip

To freeze, let meatballs cool in jelly-roll pan on wire rack. When cool, freeze in pan. Place frozen meatballs in large self-sealing plastic bag and freeze for up to 1 month. Thaw in refrigerator overnight. Or, remove meatballs from bag and place on a microwave-safe plate. Microwave on Medium (50 percent power) for 2 to 4 minutes, until just thawed.

Radiatore with Sweet-and-Spicy Picadillo Sauce

A zesty Spanish dish of ground beef, spices, raisins, and tomatoes, picadillo is traditionally served over rice. But, as this recipe shows, it's spectacularly good over pasta.

PREP 10 minutes **COOK** 15 minutes **MAKES** 6 main-dish servings

1 package (16 ounces) radiatore or corkscrew pasta

1 teaspoon olive oil

1 small onion, finely chopped

2 garlic cloves, crushed with garlic press

$\frac{1}{4}$ teaspoon ground cinnamon

$\frac{1}{8}$ to $\frac{1}{4}$ teaspoon ground red pepper (cayenne)

$\frac{3}{4}$ pound ground beef

$\frac{1}{2}$ teaspoon salt

1 can (14$\frac{1}{2}$ ounces) whole tomatoes in puree

$\frac{1}{2}$ cup dark seedless raisins

$\frac{1}{4}$ cup salad olives, drained, or chopped pimento-stuffed olives

chopped fresh parsley leaves for garnish

1. In large saucepot, cook pasta as label directs.

2. Meanwhile, in nonstick 12-inch skillet heat olive oil over medium heat until hot. Add onion and cook 5 minutes or until tender, stirring frequently. Stir in garlic, cinnamon, and ground red pepper; cook 30 seconds. Increase heat to medium-high; add ground beef and salt and cook 5 minutes or until beef begins to brown, stirring frequently. Spoon off fat if necessary. Stir in tomatoes with their puree, raisins, and olives, breaking up tomatoes with side of spoon, and cook about 5 minutes longer or until sauce thickens slightly.

3. When pasta has cooked to desired doneness, remove *1 cup pasta cooking water*. Drain pasta and return to saucepot. Add ground-beef mixture and reserved pasta cooking water; toss well. Garnish with chopped parsley to serve.

EACH SERVING About 470 calories | 20 g protein | 71 g carbohydrate | 11 g total fat (4 g saturated) | 35 mg cholesterol | 775 mg sodium.

Mafalda with Veal and Rosemary

Italian cooks swear by rosemary—in fact some claim that, after parsley, it's the most popular herb in Italian kitchens. Combined with tender veal, it's *"molto bene,"* or very good.

PREP 15 minutes **COOK** about 20 minutes **MAKES** 6 main-dish servings

1 tablespoon olive oil	1/2 cup dry white wine
1 medium onion, finely chopped	1 can (14 1/2 to 16 ounces) tomatoes
1 garlic clove, minced	1 tablespoon butter or margarine
1/2 teaspoon dried rosemary leaves, crumbled	1 package (16 ounces) mafalda or spaghetti
1 pound ground veal	1/2 cup chopped fresh flat-leaf parsley
1 teaspoon salt	fresh rosemary for garnish
1/4 teaspoon ground black pepper	

1. In 12-inch skillet, heat olive oil over medium-high heat until hot. Add onion and cook until almost tender, about 3 minutes, stirring often. Stir in garlic and rosemary and cook 30 seconds.

2. Increase heat to high. Add veal, salt, and pepper and cook, stirring often, 5 to 7 minutes, until veal browns. Add wine and cook until almost evaporated, stirring to loosen brown bits. Stir in tomatoes with their juice, breaking up tomatoes with side of spoon; heat to boiling. Boil 5 minutes, stirring occasionally. Remove skillet from heat; stir in butter.

3. Meanwhile, in large saucepot, cook pasta as label directs. Drain pasta; return to saucepot. Add veal mixture and parsley; toss to coat. Garnish with fresh rosemary.

EACH SERVING About 455 calories | 26 g protein | 62 g carbohydrate | 11 g total fat (3 g saturated) | 62 mg cholesterol | 665 mg sodium.

Whole-Wheat Spaghetti with Fontina and Ham

A favorite combination—ham and cheese—tastes great tossed with pasta. If your supermarket doesn't carry Fontina, you can substitute Gruyère.

PREP 10 minutes   **COOK** 20 minutes   **MAKES** 4 main-dish servings

1 package (16 ounces) whole-wheat spaghetti

2 tablespoons olive oil

2 bunches green onions, sliced diagonally ½ inch thick

1 garlic clove, crushed with garlic press

½ teaspoon salt

¼ teaspoon crushed red pepper

1 cup chicken broth

4 ounces Fontina cheese, shredded (1 cup)

4 ounces sliced cooked ham (preferably baked), cut into 2" by ¼" strips

1. In large saucepot, cook pasta as label directs.

2. Meanwhile, in nonstick 12-inch skillet, heat oil over medium-high heat until hot. Add green onions and cook 2 to 3 minutes, until lightly golden, stirring occasionally. Add garlic, salt, and crushed red pepper and cook 30 seconds, stirring. Stir in chicken broth and heat to boiling.

3. Drain spaghetti; return to saucepot. Add broth mixture, cheese, and ham, and toss well to coat.

EACH SERVING About 640 calories | 31 g protein | 92 g carbohydrate | 20 g total fat (8 g saturated) | 48 mg cholesterol | 1,290 mg sodium.

Pasta with Spring Vegetables and Ham

Enjoy a seasonal classic—spaghetti tossed with thin strips of sautéed veggies in a lightly spiced broth. Using a pasta cooker makes draining spaghetti a breeze. Just lift the colander insert up and out, shake it, and *voilà*.

PREP 15 minutes   **COOK** 30 minutes   **MAKES** 4 main-dish servings

4 medium carrots (about 12 ounces), peeled

4 small zucchini (about 1¾ pounds)

1 tablespoon olive oil

1 large onion, thinly sliced

1 garlic clove, crushed with garlic press

½ teaspoon freshly grated lemon peel

¼ teaspoon dried thyme

⅛ teaspoon crushed red pepper

1 cup chicken broth

¾ teaspoon salt

1 package (16 ounces) thin spaghetti

4 ounces deli ham in 1 piece, cut into 3" by ¼" strips

1. Following manufacturer's directions, use V-slicer or mandoline (see Tip) fitted with thin julienne blade to slice carrots and zucchini lengthwise into matchstick-thin strips; set aside.

2. In nonstick 12-inch skillet, heat olive oil over medium heat until hot. Add onion and cook 15 minutes, stirring occasionally with heatproof spatula. Add garlic, lemon peel, thyme, and crushed red pepper, and cook 1 minute, stirring. Add carrots and cook 5 minutes, stirring occasionally.

> **GH Test Kitchen Tip**
>
> If you don't have a V-slicer or mandoline, buy carrots that are precut into julienne slices. For the zucchini, use a chef's knife to cut it into very thin strips.

Increase heat to medium-high; add zucchini and cook 8 minutes or until all vegetables are tender, stirring occasionally. Stir in broth and salt; heat through.

3. Meanwhile, in large pasta cooker with colander insert, cook spaghetti as the label directs. Lift colander insert out of pasta cooker and drain excess water. In large bowl, toss spaghetti with vegetable mixture and ham.

EACH SERVING About 575 calories | 24 g protein | 101 g carbohydrate | 9 g total fat (2 g saturated) | 15 mg cholesterol | 795 mg sodium.

Gnocchi with Ham and Asparagus

A luscious mushroom sauce transforms gnocchi into a sumptuous meal—and it takes just 15 minutes to prepare! When buying asparagus, look for tight tips and a bright green color.

PREP 15 minutes   **COOK** 15 minutes   **MAKES** 6 main-dish servings

1 package (16 ounces) gnocchi or medium shell pasta

2 tablespoons butter or margarine

1 medium onion, chopped

4 ounces sliced smoked ham, cut into thin strips

1 package (8 ounces) sliced mushrooms

1 pound asparagus, trimmed and cut into 2-inch pieces

1 cup reduced-sodium chicken broth

$\frac{1}{2}$ cup heavy or whipping cream

$\frac{1}{8}$ teaspoon ground black pepper

grated Parmesan cheese (optional)

1. In large saucepot, cook pasta as label directs.

2. Meanwhile, in 10-inch skillet, melt butter over medium-high heat. Add onion and ham and cook, stirring occasionally, 5 minutes or until onion is tender.

3. Add mushrooms and cook until mushrooms are tender and liquid has evaporated, about 5 minutes. Stir in asparagus, chicken broth, heavy or whipping cream, and black pepper; heat to boiling over high heat, stirring. Boil 3 to 5 minutes, until the asparagus is tender.

4. Drain pasta; return to saucepot. Add mushroom mixture; toss well. Serve with Parmesan cheese, if you like.

EACH SERVING About 435 calories | 17 g protein | 62 g carbohydrate | 13 g total fat (6 g saturated) | 38 mg cholesterol | 455 mg sodium.

Spaghetti all'Amatriciana

A spicy pairing of pancetta and red chiles gives this pasta classic distinctive taste. It's named for the town of Amatrice, near Rome.

PREP 10 minutes   COOK 45 minutes   MAKES 4 main-dish servings

I tablespoon olive oil

4 ounces sliced pancetta, chopped

I small onion, chopped

I garlic clove, finely chopped

¼ teaspoon crushed red pepper

I can (28 ounces) plum tomatoes

½ teaspoon salt

I package (16 ounces) spaghetti or rigatoni

¼ cup chopped fresh parsley

1. In nonreactive 5-quart Dutch oven, heat oil over medium heat. Add pancetta and cook, stirring, until lightly browned, about 5 minutes. Stir in onion and cook until tender, about 3 minutes. Stir in garlic and crushed red pepper; cook 15 seconds. Add tomatoes with their juice and salt; heat to boiling, breaking up tomatoes with side of spoon. Reduce heat and simmer, stirring occasionally, 30 minutes.

2. Meanwhile, in large saucepot, cook pasta as label directs. Drain. In warm serving bowl, toss pasta with sauce and parsley.

GH Test Kitchen Tip

Pancetta, an Italian bacon, is cured in a mixture of salt and spices. Unlike American bacon, it is not smoked so its flavor is somewhat milder. Look for it in Italian markets, specialty meats shops, or large supermarkets. If you can't find it, use bacon.

Spaghetti with Sausage and Pepper Sauce

Sweet peppers and salty sausage make a fabulous duo. We've served it over spaghetti, but you could also use penne or shells.

PREP 20 minutes   COOK 30 minutes   MAKES 4 main-dish servings

8 ounces sweet Italian-sausage links, casings removed

2 small green, red, or yellow peppers, sliced ¼ inch thick

1 small onion, cut into ½-inch pieces

2 garlic cloves, crushed with garlic press

1 can (28 ounces) whole tomatoes in juice

2 tablespoons tomato paste

½ teaspoon salt

¼ teaspoon coarsely ground black pepper

2 tablespoons chopped fresh basil or parsley

1 package (16 ounces) spaghetti or other favorite pasta

1. Heat a 4-quart saucepan over medium-high heat until hot. Add sausage, peppers, and onion, and cook until meat is browned and peppers are tender, about 10 minutes, stirring occasionally and breaking up sausage with side of spoon. Pour off drippings from saucepan, leaving sausage and vegetables in pan.

2. Stir in garlic, and cook 1 minute. Stir in tomatoes with their juice, tomato paste, salt, and black pepper; heat to boiling over high heat, stirring to break up tomatoes. Reduce heat to medium; cook, stirring occasionally, 15 minutes. Stir in basil.

3. While sauce is simmering, cook pasta as label directs. Drain.

4. To serve, in large bowl, toss the hot pasta with the sauce.

EACH SERVING ABOUT 640 calories | 26 g protein | 105 g carbohydrate | 13 g total fat (4 g saturated) | 33 mg cholesterol | 990 mg sodium.

SPAGHETTI WITH BACON AND HOT PEPPER SAUCE Omit sausage and peppers. Heat saucepan over medium heat and cook **4 slices bacon, cut into 1 inch pieces,** with onion until bacon is browned and onion is tender, about 10 minutes, stirring occasionally. Pour off drippings from pan, leaving bacon and onion. Complete and serve as in Steps 2 through 4, stirring in ⅛ **to** ¼ **teaspoon crushed red pepper** with garlic and reducing salt to ¼ teaspoon.

EACH SERVING About 515 calories | 19 g protein | 97 g carbohydrate |
6 g total fat (1 g saturated) | 15 mg cholesterol | 570 mg sodium.

Pasta with Sausage and Radicchio

Some like it hot; some like it made with sweet sausage. Either way, this hearty dish is delicious and sure to please.

PREP 15 minutes   **COOK** 30 minutes   **MAKES** 6 main-dish servings

8 ounces sweet and/or hot Italian-sausage links, casings removed

1 jumbo onion (1 pound), cut in half and thinly sliced

3 tablespoons water

1 large head radicchio (about 8 ounces), cut in half and thinly sliced

¼ teaspoon salt

¼ teaspoon coarsely ground black pepper

1 package (16 ounces) penne pasta

1 cup loosely packed fresh basil leaves, chopped

1. Heat nonstick 12-inch skillet over medium-high heat until hot. Add sausage and cook about 7 minutes or until browned, stirring frequently to break up sausage. With slotted spoon, transfer sausage to large serving bowl.

2. Add onion and water to drippings in skillet, and cook about 15 minutes or until onion is soft and golden, stirring occasionally. Reserve ¾ cup sliced radicchio. Add remaining radicchio to skillet with onion; cook 5 minutes.

3. Meanwhile, in large saucepot, cook pasta as label directs. Drain, reserving *1 cup pasta cooking water*. Transfer pasta and reserved cooking water to bowl with sausage; toss with onion mixture, salt, and pepper. Top with basil and reserved radicchio; toss to serve.

EACH SERVING About 450 calories | 17 g protein | 65 g carbohydrate | 13 g total fat (5 g saturated) | 29 mg cholesterol | 485 mg sodium.

Mafalda with Lamb and Mint

Morocco was the inspiration for the spice mix in this dish. Ruffle-edged mafalda makes a nice change from flat pasta (see photo on page 37).

PREP 15 minutes   COOK 25 minutes   MAKES 6 main-dish servings

1 tablespoon olive oil

1 large onion, cut into ¼-inch dice

1 medium red pepper, cut into ¼-inch dice

12 ounces ground lamb

3 garlic cloves, minced

2 teaspoons dried mint

2 teaspoons ground coriander

¾ teaspoon salt

½ teaspoon ground red pepper (cayenne)

1 can (28 ounces) whole tomatoes in juice

3 tablespoons tomato paste

12 ounces mafalda noodles or fettuccine

½ cup loosely packed fresh parsley leaves, chopped

fresh parsley for garnish

1. In nonstick 12-inch skillet, heat oil over medium heat until hot. Add onion and diced red pepper, and cook 10 minutes or until lightly browned and almost tender, stirring occasionally. Increase heat to medium-high; add lamb, garlic, mint, coriander, salt, and ground red pepper and cook 8 minutes or until browned, stirring occasionally.

2. Stir in tomatoes with their juices and tomato paste, breaking up tomatoes with side of spoon; heat to boiling. Reduce heat to medium and simmer, uncovered, 5 minutes.

3. Meanwhile, in large saucepot, cook mafalda as label directs. Drain mafalda; return to saucepot. Add lamb mixture and chopped parsley, and toss well to coat. Garnish with parsley.

EACH SERVING About 440 calories | 19 g protein | 55 g carbohydrate | 17 g total fat (6 g saturated) | 41 mg cholesterol | 780 mg sodium.

Penne with Salmon and Asparagus

A spring evening, when the first asparagus appear in the market, is the perfect time to make this enticing dish. Serve a dessert of fresh strawberries topped with brown-sugar-sweetened sour cream flavored with a little vanilla.

PREP 15 minutes   **COOK** 15 minutes   **MAKES** 6 main-dish servings

1 package (16 ounces) penne rigate or bow ties

3 teaspoons olive oil

1 pound asparagus, trimmed and cut into 2-inch pieces

1/2 teaspoon salt

1/4 teaspoon coarsely ground black pepper

1 large shallot, finely chopped (1/4 cup)

1/3 cup dry white wine

1 cup low-sodium chicken broth

1 skinless salmon fillet (1 pound), cut crosswise into thirds, then lengthwise into 1/4-inch-thick slices

1 tablespoon chopped fresh tarragon

1. In large saucepot, cook pasta as label directs. Drain.

2. Meanwhile, in nonstick 12-inch skillet, heat 2 teaspoons oil over medium-high heat. Add asparagus, salt, and pepper and cook until asparagus is almost tender-crisp, about 5 minutes. Add shallot and remaining 1 teaspoon oil; cook, stirring constantly, 2 minutes longer. Add wine; heat to boiling over high heat. Stir in broth and heat to boiling. Place salmon slices in skillet; cover and cook until just opaque throughout, 2 to 3 minutes. Remove skillet from heat; stir in tarragon. In warm serving bowl, toss pasta with asparagus mixture.

EACH SERVING About 460 calories | 27 g protein | 60 g carbohydrate | 12 g total fat (2 g saturated) | 45 mg cholesterol | 404 mg sodium.

> ### GH Test Kitchen Tip
> If you can't find fresh tarragon, substitute 1 teaspoon dried: just crumble it with your fingers to release the flavor.

Shells with Smoked Trout and Chives

A lemony cream sauce cloaks smoky fish. Toss with green beans and pasta and dinner is on!

PREP 15 minutes COOK 15 minutes MAKES 6 main-dish servings

1 whole smoked trout (about 6 ounces) or other smoked fish

½ cup half-and-half or light cream

½ teaspoon grated lemon peel

¼ teaspoon coarsely ground black pepper

¼ teaspoon salt

4 tablespoons chopped fresh chives or scallion greens

1 package (16 ounces) medium shell pasta or linguine

12 ounces green beans, trimmed

fresh chives for garnish

1. Remove head, tail, skin, and bones from trout and discard. Separate flesh into 1-inch pieces. In 2-quart saucepan, heat half-and-half, lemon peel, pepper, salt, and 1 tablespoon chopped chives over low heat to simmering. Remove saucepan from heat; cover and keep warm.

2. In large saucepot, cook pasta as label directs. If you like, cut green beans crosswise in half. After pasta has cooked 5 minutes, add green beans to pasta cooking water and continue cooking.

3. When pasta and beans have cooked to desired doneness, remove ½ cup *pasta cooking water*. Drain pasta and beans; return to saucepot. Add half-and-half mixture, trout, reserved pasta cooking water, and remaining 3 tablespoons chopped chives; toss well. Garnish with chives.

EACH SERVING About 350 calories | 15 g protein | 62 g carbohydrate | 5 g total fat (2 g saturated) | 10 mg cholesterol | 360 mg sodium.

> ### GH Test Kitchen Tip
> The saltiness of smoked fish can vary considerably, so taste first before adding the salt in Step 1.

Seafood-Stuffed Shells

Easy to serve and easy to eat—these shrimp-and-scrod-filled shells make a terrific party dish.

🕐 **PREP** 1 hour 15 minutes **BAKE** 20 minutes **MAKES** 10 main-dish servings

30 jumbo pasta shells

1 tablespoon olive oil

1 small onion, chopped

2 garlic cloves, minced

1 bottle (8 ounces) clam juice

1 can (28 ounces) whole tomatoes in puree

2 tablespoons tomato paste

1 teaspoon sugar

¼ teaspoon crushed red pepper

⅓ cup heavy or whipping cream

1 pound medium shrimp, shelled, deveined, and coarsely chopped

1 pound scrod fillet, coarsely chopped

1 package (10 ounces) frozen peas

BREAD-CRUMB TOPPING

1 tablespoon olive oil

1 garlic clove, crushed with side of chef's knife

2 slices firm white bread, torn into ¼-inch pieces

1. In large saucepot, cook pasta as label directs. Drain pasta and rinse with cold running water to stop cooking; drain again. Arrange shells in single layer on waxed paper and set aside.

2. Meanwhile, in 4-quart saucepan, heat olive oil over medium heat until hot. Add onion and cook until tender, about 5 minutes. Add garlic and cook 1 minute longer, stirring frequently. Add clam juice and cook 7 minutes over high heat until reduced to ½ cup. Stir in tomatoes with their puree, breaking up tomatoes with side of spoon. Add tomato paste, sugar, and crushed red pepper; heat to boiling. Reduce heat to low; partially cover and simmer about 20 minutes, stirring occasionally. Stir in cream and cook 2 minutes longer; remove saucepan from heat.

3. Transfer 1 cup tomato sauce to 3-quart saucepan. Add shrimp and scrod, and cook over medium-high heat until seafood just turns opaque throughout, about 5 minutes, gently stirring occasionally. Remove the saucepan from heat; stir equal amounts of frozen peas into both saucepans.

4. Preheat oven to 400°F. Fill each pasta shell with 2 heaping tablespoons seafood mixture and place in 13" by 9" glass baking dish. Pour tomato sauce over stuffed shells.

5. Prepare bread-crumb topping: In nonstick 10-inch skillet, heat olive oil and garlic over medium heat. Add bread and cook until it is golden, about 5 minutes, stirring often. Discard garlic.

6. Spoon bread crumbs over stuffed shells. Bake 20 minutes or until hot and bubbly.

EACH SERVING About 325 calories | 23 g protein | 38 g carbohydrate | 9 g total fat (3 g saturated) | 87 mg cholesterol | 450 mg sodium.

Fusilli Puttanesca

We've used tuna instead of anchovies in this tasty no-cook twist on traditional puttanesca sauce. For best flavor use extravirgin olive oil.

PREP 15 minutes **COOK** about 15 minutes **MAKES** 6 main-dish servings

1 package (16 ounces) fusilli or corkscrew pasta

3 tablespoons capers, drained and chopped

3 tablespoons minced shallot

2 tablespoons red wine vinegar

1 tablespoon olive oil

½ teaspoon grated lemon peel

½ teaspoon salt

¼ teaspoon coarsely ground black pepper

1 can (6 ounces) light tuna in olive oil

2 medium bunches watercress, tough stems removed

½ cup loosely packed fresh basil leaves, chopped

1. In large saucepot, cook pasta as label directs.

2. Meanwhile, in a large bowl, with fork, stir capers, shallot, red wine vinegar, olive oil, lemon peel, salt, and black pepper until well mixed. Add undrained tuna and watercress; toss well.

3. When pasta has cooked to desired doneness, remove *½ cup pasta cooking water*. Drain pasta and return to saucepot. Add tuna mixture, reserved pasta cooking water, and basil; toss well.

EACH SERVING About 375 calories | 17 g protein | 58 g carbohydrate | 8 g total fat (1 g saturated) | 4 mg cholesterol | 540 mg sodium.

Pasta Niçoise

The classic French composed salad that features tuna, tomatoes, and green beans—*salade niçoise*—is the inspiration for this dish. With the addition of cavatappi, a short spiral pasta, it becomes a wonderfully easy one-dish meal. You can serve it warm or at room temperature.

PREP 15 minutes   **COOK** 15 minutes   **MAKES** 6 main-dish servings

salt

1 package (16 ounces) cavatappi or radiatore pasta

1 pound red potatoes, cut into ¾-inch chunks

1 pound green beans, trimmed and each cut crosswise in half

2 lemons

¾ cup chicken broth

¼ cup olive oil

2 teaspoons Dijon mustard

½ teaspoon ground black pepper

2 anchovies, minced

1 garlic clove, crushed with garlic press

1 can (12 ounces) solid white tuna packed in water, drained

1 cup loosely packed fresh parsley leaves, chopped

⅔ cup grated Parmesan cheese

1. Heat large saucepot of *salted water* to boiling over high heat. Add pasta and potatoes; heat to boiling. Cook 2 minutes; add green beans and cook 6 minutes longer or until pasta and vegetables are tender. Drain well.

2. Meanwhile, from lemons, grate 1 teaspoon peel and squeeze 3 tablespoons juice.

3. In small bowl, with wire whisk or fork, mix lemon peel, lemon juice, broth, oil, mustard, pepper, anchovies, and garlic.

4. Arrange pasta, potatoes, beans, and tuna on platter. Drizzle with dressing; sprinkle with parsley and Parmesan.

EACH SERVING About 570 calories | 31 g protein | 78 g carbohydrate | 15 g total fat (4 g saturated) | 31 mg cholesterol | 745 mg sodium.

Linguine with White Clam Sauce

Fresh clams are surprisingly easy to prepare. And they taste fabulous tossed with sautéed garlic, parsley, and pasta with just a hint of red pepper.

PREP 15 minutes   **COOK** 30 minutes   **MAKES** 6 main-dish servings

½ cup dry white wine

2 dozen littleneck clams, scrubbed (see Tip)

1 package (16 ounces) linguine or spaghetti

¼ cup olive oil

1 large garlic clove, finely chopped

¼ teaspoon crushed red pepper

¼ cup chopped fresh parsley

1. In nonreactive 5-quart Dutch oven, heat wine to boiling over high heat. Add clams; cover and cook until clams open, 5 to 10 minutes, transferring clams to bowl as they open. Discard any clams that have not opened.

2. Strain clam broth through sieve lined with paper towels; set aside. When cool enough to handle, remove clams from shells and coarsely chop. Discard shells.

3. Meanwhile, in large saucepot, cook the pasta as label directs. Drain.

4. Add oil, garlic, and crushed red pepper to same clean Dutch oven. Cook over medium heat, stirring occasionally, just until garlic turns golden. Stir in parsley, clams, and clam broth; heat just to simmering. Add pasta to Dutch oven and toss until combined.

EACH SERVING About 427 calories | 19 g protein | 59 g carbohydrate | 11 g total fat (1 g saturated) | 24 mg cholesterol | 111 mg sodium.

GH Test Kitchen Tip

With a stiff-bristled brush or other sturdy scrubber, clean clams well under cold running water to remove sand.

Linguine with Asian-Style Clam Sauce

Our luscious, lemony version of the classic white clam sauce is lightly accented with fresh ginger.

🕐 PREP 30 minutes   COOK 30 minutes   MAKES 4 main-dish servings

1 package (16 ounces) linguine or spaghetti

3 tablespoons olive oil

3 garlic cloves, crushed with side of chef's knife

1 tablespoon grated, peeled fresh ginger

1/4 teaspoon crushed red pepper

3 dozen littleneck clams, scrubbed (see Tip page 64)

1 bottle (8 ounces) clam juice

1/2 cup dry white wine

3 strips (3" by 3/4" each) lemon peel, cut lengthwise into thin slivers

2 tablespoons butter or olive oil

1/4 cup chopped fresh cilantro leaves

1. In saucepot, cook pasta as label directs. Drain linguine reserving *3/4 cup pasta cooking water*. Return linguine to saucepot.

2. Meanwhile, in nonstick 12-inch skillet, heat olive oil over medium-high heat until hot. Add garlic and cook until golden. Add ginger and crushed red pepper; cook 30 seconds, stirring. To skillet, add clams, clam juice, wine, and lemon peel; heat to boiling. Reduce heat to medium; cover and cook 10 to 15 minutes, until clams open, removing clams to bowl as they open. Discard any clams that do not open. Stir butter or olive oil and reserved pasta cooking water into broth in skillet.

3. Stir sauce and cilantro into saucepot with linguine; heat to boiling over high heat. Reduce heat to low; cook 1 minute. Add clams; cover and heat through.

EACH SERVING About 660 calories | 30 g protein | 90 g carbohydrate | 19 g total fat (5 g saturated) | 55 mg cholesterol | 450 mg sodium.

GH Test Kitchen Tip

Mussels, tiny Manila clams, or cockles would work well here, too. Use 1 pound for each dozen clams called for in the recipe.

Linguine with Broccoli and Clams

We lightened the classic clam sauce, then added broccoli to make a healthful one-dish meal. Serve with crusty bread to soak up the juices.

PREP 30 minutes **COOK** 20 minutes **MAKES** 4 main-dish servings

½ cup dry white wine

2 dozen littleneck or small cherrystone clams, scrubbed (see Tip page 64)

½ to ¾ cup water

salt

6 cups broccoli flowerets (15 ounces)

1 package (1 pound) linguine or spaghetti

1 tablespoon olive oil

2 garlic cloves, minced

¼ teaspoon coarsely ground black pepper

⅛ to ¼ teaspoon crushed red pepper

¼ cup loosely packed fresh parsley leaves, chopped

1. In deep 12-inch skillet, heat wine to boiling over high heat; add clams and cook 5 to 10 minutes, covered, removing clams to large bowl as they begin to open. Discard any unopened clams. Line large sieve with 2 layers of paper towels and set over medium bowl. Pour clam cooking broth from skillet into sieve; reserve strained broth. (You should have about 1 cup broth. Add enough water to equal 1½ cups.) Remove clams from shells (reserve a few in the shell for garnish if you like), adding any clam juices to the reserved broth. Coarsely chop the clams.

2. In large saucepot of *boiling salted water*, cook broccoli 4 to 6 minutes, until almost tender. With slotted spoon or metal strainer, transfer broccoli to bowl; do not discard cooking water. Rinse broccoli with cold running water to stop cooking.

3. In same saucepot of boiling water, prepare pasta as label directs.

4. Meanwhile, clean skillet and wipe dry. Heat olive oil over medium heat until hot. Add garlic and cook 30 seconds, stirring. Add broccoli flowerets, black pepper, red pepper, clams, and reserved broth to skillet, and heat through, stirring gently.

5. Drain pasta. In large serving bowl, toss hot pasta with broccoli mixture. Add reserved clams in shells and sprinkle with parsley before serving.

EACH SERVING About 520 calories | **24 g protein** | **91 g carbohydrate** | **6 g total fat (1 g saturated)** | **18 mg cholesterol** | **360 mg sodium.**

Orzo Paella

This impressive shellfish-and-pasta meal makes a great party dish, and you can serve it right out of the Dutch oven it was made in, so there's very little cleanup.

PREP 20 minutes   COOK 1 hour 10 minutes   MAKES 6 main-dish servings

1 dozen medium mussels

1 dozen littleneck clams

1¾ cups orzo (rice-shaped pasta)

12 ounces green beans, trimmed and cut into 1½ inch pieces

1 tablespoon olive oil

1 large onion, chopped

1 large green pepper, cut into ¾-inch pieces

1 pound hot Italian-sausage links

1 can (14½ to 16 ounces) tomatoes

1 jar or can (12 to 15 ounces) white clam sauce for pasta

1. With stiff brush, scrub mussels and clams in running cold water to remove any sand. Remove beards from mussels; set aside.

2. In saucepot, prepare orzo as label directs but do not use salt in water. Add green beans to pot with orzo for the last 5 minutes of cooking. Drain orzo and beans; set aside.

3. Meanwhile, in 3½-quart Dutch oven, heat oil over medium heat until hot. Add onion and pepper and cook 10 to 15 minutes until tender and lightly browned; transfer to small bowl. In same Dutch oven, heat sausages and ¼ cup *water* to boiling over medium-high heat. Cover and cook 5 minutes. Remove cover; reduce heat to medium and continue cooking, turning sausages frequently, until water evaporates and sausages are well browned, about 15 minutes. Transfer the sausages to plate. Cut each sausage diagonally in half. Discard any fat in Dutch oven.

4. In same Dutch oven, heat tomatoes with their liquid to boiling over high heat, breaking up tomatoes with side of spoon. Add mussels and clams. Reduce heat to medium-low, cover, and simmer 5 to 10 minutes until shells open. Transfer mussels and clams to medium bowl; discard any that do not open.

5. Add clam sauce, orzo, green beans, and onion mixture to Dutch oven. Heat over medium-high heat until mixture is hot. Add mussels, clams, and sausage to Dutch oven, and heat through.

EACH SERVING About 565 calories | **30 g protein** | **58 g carbohydrate** | **24 g total fat (6 g saturated)** | **66 mg cholesterol** | **960 mg sodium.**

Linguine with Red Clam Sauce

If you can't make it to the fish market for fresh clams, substitute two cans (10 ounces each) of whole baby clams plus one-fourth of the clam liquid.

PREP 20 minutes COOK 1 hour MAKES 6 main-dish servings

Marinara Sauce (page 29)

½ cup dry white wine

2 dozen littleneck clams, scrubbed (see Tip page 64)

1 package (16 ounces) linguine

1 tablespoon butter or margarine, cut into pieces (optional)

¼ cup chopped fresh parsley

1. Prepare marinara sauce.

2. In nonreactive 12-inch skillet, heat wine to boiling over high heat. Add clams; cover and cook until clams open, 5 to 10 minutes, transferring clams to bowl as they open. Discard any clams that have not opened. Strain clam broth through sieve lined with paper towels; reserve ¼ cup. When cool enough to handle, remove clams from shells and coarsely chop. Discard shells.

3. Meanwhile, in large saucepot, cook the pasta as label directs. Drain.

4. In same clean 12-inch skillet, combine marinara sauce, reserved clam broth, and clams; cook over low heat until heated through. In warm serving bowl, toss pasta with sauce and butter or margarine, if using. Sprinkle with parsley and serve.

EACH SERVING About 429 calories | 20 g protein | 67 g carbohydrate | 9 g total fat (2 g saturated) | 29 mg cholesterol | 582 mg sodium.

Linguine with Broccoli Rabe and Anchovies

Try something new, different, and delicious—bitter broccoli rabe, salty anchovies, and sweet golden raisins. Italians call this combination *agro dolce*, which means bittersweet.

🕐 PREP 10 minutes   COOK 25 minutes   MAKES 4 main-dish servings

2 bunches broccoli rabe (1 pound each), trimmed and cut into 2-inch pieces

2 teaspoons salt

1 package (16 ounces) linguine or spaghetti

3 tablespoons olive oil

3 garlic cloves, crushed with side of chef's knife

1 can (2 ounces) anchovy fillets, drained

¼ teaspoon crushed red pepper

½ cup golden raisins

1. In 6-quart saucepot, heat *4 quarts water* to boiling over high heat. Add broccoli rabe and salt; cover and heat to boiling. Boil 5 minutes. With tongs, transfer broccoli rabe to bowl. Add pasta to saucepot and cook as label directs. Drain, reserving *¼ cup pasta cooking water*. Return pasta to pot; keep warm.

2. Meanwhile, in 12-inch skillet, heat oil over medium heat. Add garlic and cook until golden. Add anchovies and crushed red pepper; cook, stirring, just until anchovies begin to dissolve. Add broccoli rabe and raisins to anchovy mixture. Cook, stirring occasionally, until broccoli rabe is heated through and well coated with oil, about 5 minutes.

3. Add broccoli rabe mixture and reserved pasta water to pasta in saucepot; toss to combine thoroughly.

EACH SERVING About 625 calories | 23 g protein | 106 g carbohydrate | 13 g total fat (2 g saturated) | 6 mg cholesterol | 695 mg sodium.

> ### GH Test Kitchen Tip
> Broccoli rabe is most plentiful from fall to spring. It's a great way to add something fresh and green to winter menus.

Linguine with Scallops and Saffron

Sweet tender scallops in saffron-flavored cream. When buying sea scallops, look for a very pale beige or pink color and a fresh aroma. Keep them refrigerated and use within two days.

PREP 20 minutes   COOK 15 minutes   MAKES 6 main-dish servings

3 medium leeks (about 1 pound)

2 tablespoons butter or margarine

¾ teaspoon salt

¼ teaspoon coarsely ground black pepper

½ teaspoon grated orange peel

large pinch saffron threads, crumbled

¼ cup dry white wine

1 bottle (8 ounces) clam juice

1 pound sea scallops, rinsed and each cut horizontally in half

¼ cup heavy or whipping cream

1 package (16 ounces) linguine or spaghetti

½ cup loosely packed fresh parsley leaves

1. Cut off roots and tough green tops from leeks. Cut each leek lengthwise in half, then crosswise into ½-inch-wide slices. Rinse leeks in large bowl of cold water to remove sand; drain well.

2. In 12-inch skillet, melt butter or margarine over medium heat. Add leeks, salt, and pepper, and cook until leeks are soft, about 8 minutes, stirring frequently. Add orange peel and saffron and cook 2 minutes, stirring. Add wine; cook 1 minute longer. Increase heat to medium-high; add clam juice; heat to boiling. Add scallops and cook 3 to 4 minutes until opaque. Stir in cream and heat through.

GH Test Kitchen Tip

Leeks can harbor sand among their layers. Swish them thoroughly in the cleaning water to be sure all sand is removed. Transfer the cleaned leeks from the water with a slotted spoon to make certain that any sand stays at the bottom of the bowl.

3. Meanwhile, in large saucepot, cook pasta as label directs.

4. Drain pasta; return to saucepot. Add leek mixture; toss well. Sprinkle with parsley just before serving.

EACH SERVING About 440 calories | 24 g protein | 66 g carbohydrate | 9 g total fat (3 g saturated) | 40 mg cholesterol | 635 mg sodium.

Orzo with Shrimp and Feta

This sauce cooks up in minutes in your skillet. Watch the shrimp carefully and remove them as soon as they become opaque, so they don't overcook (see photo on page 57).

⬤ PREP 10 minutes   COOK 20 minutes   MAKES 4 main-dish servings

1½ cups (10 ounces) orzo (rice-shaped pasta)

1 tablespoon butter or margarine

1¼ pounds medium shrimp, shelled and deveined, with tail part of shell left on if you like

½ teaspoon salt

⅛ teaspoon coarsely ground black pepper

3 medium tomatoes, coarsely chopped

4 ounces garlic and herb-flavored feta cheese, crumbled (1 cup)

1. In saucepot, cook orzo as label directs.

2. Meanwhile, in nonstick 10-inch skillet, melt butter over medium-high heat. Add shrimp, salt, and pepper, and cook 3 to 5 minutes or until shrimp turn opaque throughout, stirring occasionally. Add tomatoes and cook 30 seconds, stirring. Remove from heat.

3. Drain orzo; toss with shrimp mixture and feta cheese.

EACH SERVING About 500 calories | 37 g protein | 60 g carbohydrate | 12 g total fat (5 g saturated) | 197 mg cholesterol | 895 mg sodium.

Bow Ties with Shrimp and Fennel

Super easy and super good. If you don't have a mortar and pestle, crush garlic with a press and place fennel seeds in a sealed plastic bag, then mash with a rolling pin.

PREP 10 minutes **COOK** 15 minutes **MAKES** 6 main-dish servings

1 package (16 ounces) bow-tie pasta

1 bag (16 ounces) frozen uncooked, shelled, and deveined extra large shrimp

1 cup frozen peas

1 small garlic clove

1 teaspoon fennel seeds

½ teaspoon salt

¼ teaspoon coarsely ground black pepper

4 ripe medium tomatoes, diced

2 tablespoons olive oil

2 ounces feta cheese, crumbled (½ cup)

1. In large saucepot, cook pasta as label directs. After pasta has cooked 12 minutes, add frozen shrimp and peas to pasta cooking water, and continue cooking 3 minutes or until pasta is done and shrimp turn opaque throughout.

2. Meanwhile, in mortar with pestle, crush garlic with fennel seeds, salt, and pepper. Transfer mixture to medium bowl and stir in tomatoes and olive oil.

3. Drain pasta and shrimp; return to saucepot. Add tomato mixture and feta cheese; toss well.

EACH SERVING About 465 calories | 29 g protein | 66 g carbohydrate | 9 g total fat (3 g saturated) | 125 mg cholesterol | 520 mg sodium.

GH Test Kitchen Tip

The delicate anise flavor of fennel seeds can enhance both sweet and savory foods. They are especially good with fish, poultry, and vegetables such as beets and cabbage, and baked goods.

Pad Thai

Go to a Thai restaurant and you're certain to find Pad Thai—a tasty mix of noodles, shrimp, peanuts, and eggs. It's surprisingly easy to make at home, just be sure to have everything in place before you start because it cooks quickly.

PREP 25 minutes **COOK** 5 minutes **MAKES** 4 main-dish servings

1 package (7 or 8 ounces) flat rice stick noodles, broken in half, or 8 ounces angel hair pasta

½ pound medium shrimp, shelled and deveined

¼ cup fresh lime juice

¼ cup Asian fish sauce (see Tip)

2 tablespoons sugar

1 tablespoon vegetable oil

2 garlic cloves, crushed with garlic press

¼ teaspoon crushed red pepper

2 large eggs, lightly beaten

6 ounces fresh bean sprouts (about 2 cups), rinsed

2 tablespoons unsalted roasted peanuts, coarsely chopped

3 green onions, thinly sliced

½ cup loosely packed cilantro leaves

lime wedges

1. In large bowl, soak rice stick noodles in *hot tap water* to cover 20 minutes. (Or, break angel hair pasta in half; cook as label directs and rinse with cold running water.)

2. Meanwhile, cut each shrimp horizontally in half. In small bowl, combine lime juice, fish sauce, and sugar. Assemble all remaining ingredients before beginning to cook.

3. Drain noodles. In a nonstick wok or 12-inch skillet, heat vegetable oil over high heat until hot but not smoking. Add shrimp, garlic, and crushed red pepper and cook, stirring, 1 minute. Add eggs and cook, stirring, 20 sec-

---

GH Test Kitchen Tip

Kept in a cool place, pungent Asian fish sauce (also called *nam pla*) will last almost indefinitely. Look for it, as well as rice stick noodles, in Asian markets and large supermarkets.

---

onds or until just set. Add noodles and cook, stirring, 2 minutes. Add lime-juice mixture, half of bean sprouts, half of peanuts, and half of green onions; cook, stirring, for 1 minute.

4. Transfer Pad Thai to platter; top with remaining bean sprouts, peanuts, and green onions. Sprinkle with cilantro leaves. Serve with lime wedges.

EACH SERVING About 395 calories | 19 g protein | 59 g carbohydrate | 9 g total fat (2 g saturated) | 172 mg cholesterol | 1,400 mg sodium.

Vermicelli with Shrimp and Broccoli

For a delicious change of pace, shrimp and broccoli are stir-fried with one of our favorite Asian spice combinations—garlic, hot red pepper, and soy sauce. Add pasta and serve.

PREP 15 minutes   COOK 15 minutes   MAKES 6 main-dish servings

1 package (16 ounces) vermicelli or thin spaghetti

1 tablespoon vegetable oil

1 pound medium shrimp, shelled and deveined, with tail part of shell left on if you like

1 tablespoon grated, peeled fresh ginger

2 garlic cloves, crushed with garlic press

¼ teaspoon crushed red pepper

2 packages (12 ounces each) broccoli flowerets

1 cup reduced-sodium chicken broth

2 tablespoons soy sauce

1 teaspoon Asian sesame oil

1. In large saucepot, cook pasta as label directs.

2. Meanwhile, in 10-inch skillet, heat vegetable oil over medium-high heat until hot. Add shrimp, ginger, garlic, and crushed red pepper. Cook, stirring, 2 minutes or just until shrimp turn opaque throughout. Transfer shrimp to bowl.

3. Add broccoli to skillet and cook, stirring, 1 minute. Stir in chicken broth and heat to boiling over high heat. Cook, uncovered, stirring often, until broccoli is just tender, about 3 minutes. Stir in soy sauce, sesame oil, and shrimp; heat through.

4. Drain pasta; return to saucepot. Add shrimp mixture; toss well.

EACH SERVING About 415 calories | 26 g protein | 65 g carbohydrate | 6 g total fat (1 g saturated) | 95 mg cholesterol | 655 mg sodium.

GH Test Kitchen Tip

If you're in a hurry, buy shelled and deveined medium-size shrimp.

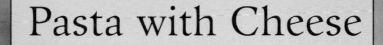

Pasta with Cheese

Lasagna Toss with Spinach and Ricotta
recipe on page 96

Corkscrews with Spring Veggies

For an easy—and yummy—main dish, toss sautéed asparagus and leeks with pasta and creamy goat cheese.

PREP 15 minutes **COOK** 15 minutes **MAKES** 4 main-dish servings

1 bunch leeks (about 1 pound)

1 package (16 ounces) corkscrew or bow-tie pasta

1 tablespoon butter or margarine

1 pound asparagus, trimmed and cut diagonally into 2-inch pieces

¾ teaspoon salt

coarsely ground black pepper

⅓ cup water

1 package (4 ounces) soft goat cheese, cut into small pieces

1. Cut off roots and leaf ends from leeks. Discard any tough outer leaves. Cut each leek lengthwise in half, then crosswise into ¼-inch-wide slices. Place leeks in large bowl of cold water; with hand, swish leeks around to remove any sand. Transfer leeks to colander. Repeat process, changing water several times, until all sand is removed. Drain well.

2. In large saucepot, cook pasta as label directs.

3. Meanwhile, in nonstick 12-inch skillet, melt butter over medium heat. Add leeks and cook until almost tender, about 5 minutes, stirring often. Stir in asparagus, salt, and ¼ teaspoon pepper; cook 5 minutes longer, stirring often. Add water; cover and cook 3 to 5 minutes, until asparagus is tender-crisp.

4. Drain pasta, reserving ¾ *cup pasta cooking water*. Return pasta to saucepot. Add asparagus mixture and pasta cooking water; toss well. Spoon into large serving bowl; sprinkle with goat cheese and black pepper.

EACH SERVING About 580 calories | 23 g protein | 96 g carbohydrate | 11 g total fat (5 g saturated) | 13 mg cholesterol | 705 mg sodium.

GH Test Kitchen Tip

Peak season for fresh asparagus is spring. Look for crisp green stalks with tips that appear tightly closed.

Fettuccine Alfredo

This luscious classic takes its name from Roman restaurateur Alfredo di Lello, who created it in the early 1900s. Be sure to use only freshly grated Parmesan cheese and, for a delicious splurge, make it authentic Italian Parmigiano-Reggiano.

◔ PREP 10 minutes COOK 25 minutes MAKES 6 accompaniment servings

I package (16 ounces) fettuccine

1½ cups heavy or whipping cream

I tablespoon butter or margarine

½ teaspoon salt

¼ teaspoon coarsely ground black pepper

¾ cup freshly grated Parmesan cheese

chopped fresh parsley

1. In large saucepot, cook pasta as label directs. Drain.

2. Meanwhile, in 2-quart saucepan, heat cream, butter or margarine, salt, and pepper to boiling over medium-high heat. Boil until sauce has thickened slightly, 2 to 3 minutes. In warm serving bowl, toss pasta with sauce and Parmesan. Sprinkle with parsley.

EACH SERVING About 558 calories | 16 g protein | 59 g carbohydrate | 29 g total fat (17 g saturated) | 96 mg cholesterol | 532 mg sodium.

GH Test Kitchen Tip

For a more delicate rendition of this dish, seek out fresh fettuccine in the refrigerated section of your supermarket.

Light Fettuccine Alfredo

For a weeknight family supper, you might prefer this low-fat version of the classic **Alfredo** sauce. We shaved off calories while keeping the sauce smooth and cheesy.

PREP 15 minutes   **COOK** 20 minutes   **MAKES** 4 main-dish servings

2 teaspoons vegetable oil

1 small onion, finely chopped

1 large garlic clove, crushed with garlic press

2 cups skim milk

1 cup chicken broth

3 tablespoons all-purpose flour

$\frac{1}{2}$ teaspoon salt

$\frac{1}{4}$ teaspoon coarsely ground black pepper

$\frac{1}{2}$ cup freshly grated Parmesan cheese

1 package (16 ounces) fettuccine

1 package (16 ounces) broccoli flowerets

1. In nonstick 12-inch skillet, heat oil over medium heat. Add onion and garlic and cook until onion is golden, about 8 minutes. In bowl, with wire whisk, whisk milk, broth, flour, salt, and pepper until smooth. Add to onion mixture and cook, stirring, until sauce has thickened and boils; boil 1 minute. Stir in Parmesan.

2. Meanwhile, in large saucepot, cook pasta as label directs. After pasta has cooked 7 minutes, add broccoli to pasta water. Cook until pasta and broccoli are done, 3 to 5 minutes longer. Drain pasta and broccoli.

3. In warm serving bowl, toss pasta and broccoli with sauce.

EACH SERVING About 613 calories | 29 g protein | 104 g carbohydrate | 9 g total fat (3 g saturated) | 12 mg cholesterol | 981 mg sodium.

Gemelli with Feta, Mint, and Olives

The tantalizing flavors of a Greek salad—feta cheese, mint, and olives—are perfect with pasta. Taste your olives before making the sauce—if they're very briny, you may want to omit or reduce the amount of lemon juice.

🕒 **PREP** 15 minutes   **COOK** 15 minutes
MAKES 4 main-dish or 8 accompaniment servings

1 package (16 ounces) gemelli or penne pasta

4 ounces feta cheese, crumbled (1 cup)

¼ cup Kalamata olives, pitted and sliced

¼ cup chopped fresh mint leaves

2 tablespoons extravirgin olive oil

1 tablespoon fresh lemon juice

⅛ teaspoon ground black pepper

1 bunch spinach (10 to 12 ounces), tough stems removed and leaves torn

1. In large saucepot, cook pasta as label directs.

2. Meanwhile, in medium bowl, combine feta cheese, Kalamata olives, mint, olive oil, lemon juice, and black pepper.

3. Drain pasta; return to saucepot. Add feta mixture and spinach; toss well.

EACH MAIN-DISH SERVING About 595 calories | 20 g protein | 90 g carbohydrate | 17 g total fat (6 g saturated) | 25 mg cholesterol | 640 mg sodium.

GH Test Kitchen Tip

To pit an olive, use a cherry pitter or place olive on a work surface and press firmly with the flat side of a large knife. The pit should slip out easily.

Cheesy Pasta and Mushrooms

Thanks to supermarket-sliced mushrooms and herbed cheese, this dish is a breeze to prepare.

🕐 PREP 15 minutes   COOK 20 minutes   MAKES 4 main-dish servings

12 ounces campanelle or bow-tie pasta

2 tablespoons butter or margarine

1 pound assorted sliced mushrooms

½ teaspoon salt

¼ teaspoon coarsely ground black pepper

1 cup chicken broth

1 package (4.4 ounces) light garlic-and-herb spreadable cheese

1. In large saucepot, cook pasta as label directs.

2. Meanwhile, in nonstick 12-inch skillet, melt butter over medium-high heat. Add mushrooms; sprinkle with salt and pepper. Cook mushrooms 12 minutes or until lightly browned, stirring occasionally. Stir in broth and cheese; heat through, stirring to combine.

3. Drain pasta. In large serving bowl, toss pasta with mushroom mixture.

EACH SERVING About 470 calories | 17 g protein | 72 g carbohydrate | 13 g total fat (5 g saturated) | 22 mg cholesterol | 900 mg sodium.

GH Test Kitchen Tip

Have fun trying different combinations of mushrooms. We used 2 packages (4 ounces each) sliced wild mushroom blend and 1 package (8 ounces) sliced white mushrooms.

Creamy Rigatoni with Spinach

Ricotta is the base for this simple, no-cook pasta sauce. We used part-skim to cut the fat and make a more healthful family meal.

PREP 10 minutes **COOK** 20 minutes **MAKES** 6 main-dish servings

1 package (16 ounces) rigatoni or ziti pasta

1 package (10 ounces) frozen chopped spinach

1 container (15 ounces) part-skim ricotta cheese

¹/₄ cup grated Parmesan cheese

10 oil-packed sun-dried tomatoes, drained and finely chopped (about ¹/₄ cup)

³/₄ teaspoon salt

1. In large saucepot, cook pasta in *boiling salted water* 5 minutes; add frozen spinach and cook 10 minutes longer or until spinach is tender and pasta is al dente. Drain well, reserving *¹/₂ cup pasta cooking water*.

2. Return pasta, spinach, and reserved cooking water to saucepot. Add ricotta, Parmesan, sun-dried tomatoes, and salt. Heat over medium-low heat, tossing until pasta is evenly coated and heated through.

EACH SERVING About 420 calories | 21 g protein | 64 g carbohydrate | 9 g total fat (5 g saturated) | 25 mg cholesterol | 580 mg sodium.

GH Test Kitchen Tip

Save the oil from the sun-dried tomatoes and use it in salad dressings.

Spaghetti with Ricotta and Peas

Smoky bacon gives crunch and sweet peas add color to this cheesy sauce. To minimize clean up, the peas are cooked in the pot with the pasta.

 PREP 10 minutes   COOK 10 minutes   MAKES 4 main-dish servings

4 slices bacon

1 medium onion, finely chopped

1 pound thin spaghetti or vermicelli

1 package (10 ounces) frozen peas

1 container (15 ounces) part-skim ricotta cheese

½ cup grated Pecorino Romano or Parmesan cheese

½ teaspoon salt

¼ teaspoon coarsely ground black pepper

1. In 12-inch skillet, cook bacon over medium heat until browned. Transfer to paper towels. Pour off all but 1 tablespoon bacon fat from skillet. Add onion and cook until tender and golden, 8 to 10 minutes.

2. Meanwhile, in large saucepot, cook pasta as label directs.

3. During last 2 minutes of pasta cooking time, add frozen peas. When pasta is cooked to desired doneness, remove *1 cup pasta cooking water*. Drain pasta and peas. Return to saucepot and toss with onion, ricotta, Romano, salt, pepper, and reserved pasta cooking water. Crumble in bacon and toss again.

EACH SERVING About 745 calories | 37 g protein | 103 g carbohydrate | 20 g total fat (10 g saturated) | 54 mg cholesterol | 880 mg sodium.

Cavatelli with Ricotta and Fresh Tomato Sauce

Fresh, sun-ripened tomatoes bursting with juice are all it takes to make this spectacularly good yet easy Italian sauce.

PREP 5 minutes   COOK 25 minutes   MAKES 4 main-dish servings

1 bag (16 ounces) frozen cavatelli (see Tip)

1 tablespoon olive oil

1 garlic clove, crushed with garlic press

4 medium tomatoes (about 1½ pounds), diced

½ teaspoon salt

¼ teaspoon coarsely ground black pepper

¾ cup part-skim ricotta cheese

¼ cup grated Pecorino Romano or Parmesan cheese

1. In large saucepot, cook cavatelli as label directs.

2. Meanwhile, in nonstick 10-inch skillet, heat olive oil over medium heat. Add garlic and cook 1 minute, stirring. Stir in tomatoes, salt, and pepper and cook, stirring occasionally, 5 minutes or until tomatoes break up slightly.

3. Drain cavatelli; transfer to serving bowl. Stir in ricotta and Romano. Pour tomato mixture on top; toss before serving.

EACH SERVING About 455 calories | 20 g protein | 71 g carbohydrate | 11 g total fat (5 g saturated) | 40 mg cholesterol | 560 mg sodium.

GH Test Kitchen Tip

Look for cavatelli, a short, rippled pasta, in the freezer section of the supermarket. If it's not available, use frozen gnocchi.

Pesto Ravioli and Peas

With store-bought pesto and a no-cook tomato sauce, you can have dinner on the table in under 20 minutes!

PREP 10 minutes **COOK** 6 minutes **MAKES** 4 main-dish servings

1 pound refrigerated cheese ravioli

2 medium tomatoes, cut into ¼-inch dice

1 cup loosely packed fresh basil leaves, chopped

⅛ teaspoon salt

⅛ teaspoon coarsely ground black pepper

1 package (10 ounces) frozen peas

¼ cup basil pesto, store-bought or homemade (page 36)

1. In large saucepot, cook ravioli as label directs.

2. Meanwhile, in small bowl, combine tomatoes, basil, salt, and pepper; set aside.

3. Place frozen peas in colander, and drain ravioli over peas. In large serving bowl, toss the ravioli and peas with pesto; top with the tomato mixture.

EACH SERVING About 510 calories | 23 g protein | 55 g carbohydrate | 24 g total fat (9 g saturated) | 43 mg cholesterol | 705 mg sodium.

Penne with Caramelized Onions and Radicchio

Caramelizing the onion brings out its natural sweetness—a perfect complement for the slightly bitter taste of the radicchio.

PREP 15 minutes   COOK 20 minutes   MAKES 4 main-dish servings

1 large head (8 ounces) radicchio

2 teaspoons olive oil

1 jumbo onion (1 pound), thinly sliced

1 tablespoon balsamic vinegar

½ teaspoon salt

¼ teaspoon coarsely ground black pepper

1 package (16 ounces) penne or ziti pasta

1 cup frozen peas, thawed

¼ cup crumbled ricotta salata or goat cheese

1. Cut radicchio lengthwise in half. Remove core, then cut crosswise into ½-inch slices. Set aside. In nonstick 12-inch skillet, heat olive oil over medium heat until hot. Add onion and cook until browned and soft, about 15 minutes, stirring occasionally. Add vinegar, salt, and pepper and cook 1 minute longer. Increase heat to medium-high; add radicchio and cook 2 to 3 minutes, until wilted.

2. Meanwhile, in saucepot, cook penne as label directs. Drain penne, reserving ¼ *cup pasta cooking water*. Return the penne to the saucepot.

3. Add onion mixture, peas, and reserved pasta cooking water to penne; toss to mix well. Serve sprinkled with cheese.

EACH SERVING About 550 calories | 20 g protein | 104 g carbohydrate | 6 g total fat (2 g saturated) | 3 mg cholesterol | 510 mg sodium.

Pasta with Roasted Vegetables

A sprinkling of ricotta salata cheese is just right with a medley of cauliflower and red bell peppers. If your supermarket doesn't carry it, substitute feta cheese.

PREP 45 minutes   **ROAST/BAKE** 50 minutes   **MAKES** 4 main-dish servings

3 large red peppers, cut into 1-inch pieces

4 garlic cloves, peeled

2 tablespoons olive oil

½ teaspoon salt

1 large head cauliflower (about 2½ pounds), separated into 1-inch flowerets and remainder cut into 1-inch pieces

12 ounces dried cavatelli or bow-tie pasta

1 tablespoon cornstarch

1 can (14½ ounces) chicken broth

½ cup cold water

⅓ cup loosely packed fresh parsley leaves, chopped

3 tablespoons grated Parmesan cheese

¼ teaspoon ground red pepper (cayenne)

⅛ teaspoon dried thyme

4 ounces ricotta salata cheese, crumbled

1. Preheat oven to 450°F. In 15½" by 10½" jelly-roll pan, toss red-pepper pieces and garlic with 1 tablespoon olive oil and ¼ teaspoon salt. In another 15½" by 10½" jelly-roll pan or on a large cookie sheet, toss cauliflower pieces with 1 tablespoon olive oil and ¼ teaspoon salt.

2. Place pans with vegetables on 2 oven racks in oven. Roast vegetables 30 minutes or until browned, stirring halfway through roasting time and rotating pans between upper and lower racks after 15 minutes. Turn oven control to 400°F.

3. Meanwhile, in large saucepot, cook pasta as label directs.

4. In 2-quart saucepan, with wire whisk, mix cornstarch with chicken broth and cold water; heat to boiling over medium-high heat. Boil 1 minute.

5. Drain pasta and return to saucepot. Toss pasta with roasted vegetables, broth mixture, parsley, Parmesan, ground red pepper, and thyme. Transfer pasta to deep 2½-quart baking pan or casserole.

6. Bake pasta 15 minutes. Remove from oven and top with crumbled ricotta salata cheese. Bake the pasta, uncovered, 5 minutes longer or until hot.

EACH SERVING **About 560 calories | 23 g protein | 81 g carbohydrate | 17 g total fat (7 g saturated) | 29 mg cholesterol | 1,120 mg**

Bow Ties with Tomatoes, Herbs, and Lemon

A quick toss with hot pasta is the only "cooking" this sauce needs. Make it in summer when ripe tomatoes and basil are at their best.

PREP 15 minutes plus standing **COOK** 25 minutes **MAKES** 4 main-dish servings

2 pounds ripe tomatoes (6 medium), chopped

¼ cup loosely packed fresh mint leaves, chopped

¼ cup loosely packed fresh basil leaves, chopped

1 garlic clove, crushed with garlic press

1 teaspoon freshly grated lemon peel

2 tablespoons olive oil

1 teaspoon salt

¼ teaspoon ground black pepper

1 package (16 ounces) bow ties or ziti

1. In warm serving bowl, combine tomatoes, mint, basil, garlic, lemon peel, oil, salt, and pepper. Let sauce stand at room temperature at least 15 minutes or up to 1 hour to allow flavors to develop.

2. Meanwhile, in large saucepot, cook pasta as label directs. Drain. Add pasta to tomato mixture and toss well.

EACH SERVING About 536 calories | 17 g protein | 97 g carbohydrate | 9 g total fat (1 g saturated) | 0 mg cholesterol | 711 mg sodium.

GH Test Kitchen Tip

Since the tomatoes cook only briefly here, there's no need to peel them. For easiest slicing and chopping, always use a knife with a serrated edge on tomatoes.

Pasta Puttanesca with Arugula

This zesty dish is as easy as 1, 2, 3. Chop up some tomatoes, arugula, and basil; drain the pasta; and toss in a bowl with shallot vinaigrette.

⌬ PREP 15 minutes COOK 15 minutes MAKES 4 main-dish servings

1 package (16 ounces) gemelli or corkscrew pasta

1½ pounds tomatoes (about 5 medium), cut into ½-inch chunks

1 medium shallot, minced (about ¼ cup)

1 garlic clove, crushed with garlic press

2 tablespoons olive oil

2 tablespoons capers, drained and chopped

1 tablespoon red wine vinegar

½ teaspoon grated fresh lemon peel

¼ teaspoon crushed red pepper

2 bunches arugula (about 4 ounces each), tough stems removed, leaves coarsely chopped

1 cup packed fresh basil leaves, chopped

1. In large saucepot, cook pasta as label directs.

2. Meanwhile, in large serving bowl, toss tomatoes with shallot, garlic, olive oil, capers, vinegar, grated lemon peel, and crushed red pepper until well mixed.

3. Drain pasta; toss with tomato mixture in bowl. Just before serving, gently toss pasta mixture with arugula and basil until the greens are slightly wilted.

EACH SERVING About 540 calories | 18 g protein | 97 g carbohydrate | 10 g total fat (1 g saturated) | 0 cholesterol | 310 mg sodium.

Spaghetti with Roasted Tomato Sauce

Your oven does most of the work for this dish—mellowing the flavors of the garlic and tomatoes as they roast (see photo on page 30).

PREP 10 minutes plus cooling **ROAST/COOK** 1 hour
MAKES 4 main-dish servings

2 tablespoons olive oil

3 pounds ripe plum tomatoes (16 medium), cut lengthwise in half

6 garlic cloves, not peeled

1 package (16 ounces) spaghetti or linguine

¾ teaspoon salt

¼ teaspoon coarsely ground black pepper

freshly grated Pecorino Romano cheese (optional)

1. Preheat oven to 450°F. Brush jelly-roll pan with 1 tablespoon oil. Arrange tomatoes, cut side down, in pan; add garlic. Roast tomatoes and garlic until tomatoes are well browned and garlic has softened, 50 to 60 minutes.

2. When cool enough to handle, peel tomatoes over medium bowl to catch any juices. Place tomatoes in bowl; discard skins. Squeeze garlic to separate pulp from skins. Add garlic to tomatoes.

3. Meanwhile, in large saucepot, cook the pasta as label directs. Drain.

4. With back of spoon, crush tomatoes and garlic. Stir in salt, pepper, and remaining 1 tablespoon oil. Serve sauce at room temperature or transfer to saucepan and heat through over low heat. In warm serving bowl, toss pasta with sauce. Serve with Romano, if you like.

EACH SERVING About 552 calories | 17 g protein | 101 g carbohydrate | 10 g total fat (1 g saturated) | 0 mg cholesterol | 570 mg sodium.

Penne with Creamy Tomato Sauce

Based on the restaurant favorite **Penne with Vodka Sauce**, this dish is a snap to make at home. You won't actually taste the vodka; it simply helps meld the other flavors.

PREP 15 minutes   COOK 30 minutes   MAKES 4 main-dish servings

1 tablespoon olive oil

1 small onion, chopped

1 garlic clove, finely chopped

$1/8$ to $1/4$ teaspoon crushed red pepper

1 can (28 ounces) tomatoes in puree, coarsely chopped

3 tablespoons vodka (optional)

$1/2$ teaspoon salt

$1/2$ cup heavy or whipping cream

1 cup frozen peas, thawed

1 package (16 ounces) penne or rotini

$1/2$ cup loosely packed fresh basil leaves, thinly sliced

1. In nonstick 12-inch skillet, heat oil over medium heat. Add onion and cook until tender, about 5 minutes. Add garlic and crushed red pepper; cook until garlic is golden, about 30 seconds longer. Stir in tomatoes with their puree, vodka if using, and salt; heat to boiling over high heat. Reduce heat and simmer until sauce has thickened, 15 to 20 minutes. Stir in cream and peas; heat to boiling.

2. Meanwhile, in large saucepot, cook pasta as label directs. Drain. In warm serving bowl, toss pasta with sauce and sprinkle with basil.

EACH SERVING About 652 calories | 20 g protein | 107 g carbohydrate | 17 g total fat (8 g saturated) | 41 mg cholesterol | 763 mg sodium.

Thin Spaghetti with Pesto and Tomatoes

Two old favorites add up to one great meal when spaghetti with pesto is topped with a cherry-tomato salad. If you're in a hurry, you can substitute 4 ounces of prepared pesto.

PREP 30 minutes   **COOK** 6 minutes   **MAKES** 4 main-dish servings

BASIL PESTO

2 cups packed fresh basil leaves

2 garlic cloves, cut in half

2 tablespoons pine nuts (pignoli), toasted

1 teaspoon salt

$\frac{1}{8}$ teaspoon ground black pepper

$\frac{1}{4}$ cup olive oil

$\frac{1}{2}$ cup grated Parmesan cheese

CHERRY-TOMATO SALAD

1$\frac{1}{2}$ pints red and/or yellow cherry tomatoes, each cut in half (about 3$\frac{1}{2}$ cups)

$\frac{1}{2}$ small red onion, thinly sliced (about $\frac{1}{2}$ cup)

$\frac{1}{3}$ cup packed fresh basil leaves, cut into strips

1 tablespoon extravirgin olive oil

1$\frac{1}{2}$ teaspoons red wine vinegar

$\frac{1}{2}$ teaspoon salt

$\frac{1}{4}$ teaspoon ground black pepper

1 package (16 ounces) thin spaghetti

basil sprigs for garnish

1. Prepare basil pesto: In food processor with knife blade attached, blend basil, garlic, pine nuts, salt, and pepper until pureed. With processor running, gradually pour in oil until blended. Add Parmesan, pulsing to combine. Transfer pesto to small bowl. Place plastic wrap directly on pesto surface to prevent browning; set aside.

2. Prepare cherry-tomato salad: In medium bowl, mix tomatoes, onion, basil strips, oil, vinegar, salt, and pepper. Set aside.

3. In large saucepot, cook spaghetti as label directs.

4. When spaghetti has cooked to desired doneness, remove $\frac{1}{4}$ *cup pasta cooking water* and reserve. Drain spaghetti and return to saucepot. Add pesto and reserved cooking water; toss well.

5. To serve, spoon spaghetti mixture into 4 serving bowls; top with tomato salad. Garnish with basil sprigs.

EACH SERVING About 680 calories | 22 g protein | 95 g carbohydrate |
24 g total fat (5 g saturated) | 8 mg cholesterol | 1,225 mg sodium.

Pasta with Asparagus Pesto

Michael Chiarello, chef-owner of Tra Vigne restaurant in the Napa Valley and author of *The Tra Vigne Cookbook*, inspired this dish when he visited the *Good Housekeeping* test kitchen.

PREP 20 minutes   **COOK** 15 minutes   **MAKES** 4 main-dish servings

1½ pounds asparagus, trimmed

¼ cup olive oil

2 tablespoons pine nuts (pignoli), toasted

¼ teaspoon ground black pepper

1 garlic clove, crushed with garlic press

¾ cup packed fresh basil leaves

1 teaspoon salt

⅓ cup grated Pecorino Romano cheese, plus additional for serving

1 pound orecchiette or medium shell pasta

1. If using thin asparagus, cut each stalk crosswise in half; if using medium asparagus, cut stalks into 1½-inch pieces. In 12-inch skillet, heat *1 inch water* to boiling over high heat. Add asparagus and cook 5 minutes or until tender. Remove and reserve *½ cup of the asparagus cooking water*; drain the asparagus.

2. Set aside 1 cup thin asparagus stalks or ½ cup medium asparagus tips. In blender at low speed, with center part of cover removed to allow steam to escape, blend remaining asparagus with oil, pine nuts, pepper, garlic, ½ cup basil, salt, and reserved asparagus cooking water until almost smooth. Add Romano cheese and blend until well mixed.

3. Meanwhile, in large saucepot cook pasta as label directs.

4. Slice remaining ¼ cup basil leaves. Drain pasta and return to saucepot. Add asparagus sauce, sliced basil, and reserved asparagus, and toss until evenly mixed. Serve with additional Romano cheese, if you like.

EACH SERVING About 620 calories | 21 g protein | 88 g carbohydrate | 20 g total fat (4 g saturated) | 7 mg cholesterol | 830 mg sodium.

Orecchini with Savoy Cabbage and Dill

A savory cream sauce flavored with fresh dill coats sweet baby peas and thin ribbons of savoy cabbage.

PREP 10 minutes **COOK** 15 minutes
MAKES 4 main-dish or 8 accompaniment servings

I tablespoon butter or margarine

I medium onion, finely chopped

I pound savoy cabbage (about
  $\frac{1}{2}$ medium head), cored and very
  thinly sliced, with tough ribs
  discarded

$\frac{3}{4}$ teaspoon salt

I cup frozen baby peas

$\frac{1}{2}$ cup reduced-sodium chicken broth

$\frac{1}{2}$ cup heavy or whipping cream

$\frac{1}{4}$ teaspoon coarsely ground
  black pepper

$\frac{1}{4}$ cup chopped fresh dill

I package (16 ounces) orecchini or
  small shell pasta

dill sprigs for garnish

1. In 12-inch skillet, melt butter over medium-high heat. Add onion and cook, stirring often, 5 minutes, or until tender.

2. Add cabbage and salt and cook until cabbage is tender-crisp, about 5 minutes, stirring often. Stir in frozen peas, chicken broth, cream, and pepper; heat to boiling. Remove skillet from heat; stir in chopped dill.

3. Meanwhile, in large saucepot, cook orecchini as label directs.

4. Drain pasta; return to saucepot. Add cabbage mixture; toss well. Garnish with dill sprigs to serve.

EACH MAIN-DISH SERVING About 615 calories | 20 g protein |
100 g carbohydrate | 16 g total fat (8 g saturated) | 41 mg cholesterol |
760 mg sodium.

GH Test Kitchen Tip

Savoy cabbage is milder and sweeter than red or green cabbage. It makes a delicious coleslaw. Look for a head that feels heavy for its size and that shows no signs of wilting.

Creste di Gallo with Sautéed Green Onions

This intriguing pasta shape was so named because it looks like a cockscomb. Dressed in a creamy low-fat onion sauce, it works well both as a main dish or served on the side with grilled lamb chops or steak.

PREP 15 minutes   **COOK** 15 minutes
MAKES 4 main-dish or 8 accompaniment servings

1 package (16 ounces) creste di gallo or orecchiette pasta

2 tablespoons butter or margarine

4 bunches green onions, chopped

¼ teaspoon coarsely ground black pepper

⅝ teaspoon salt

1 cup reduced-sodium chicken broth

1 container (8 ounces) plain low-fat yogurt

1 small garlic clove, crushed with garlic press

green onion tops for garnish

1. In large saucepot, cook pasta as label directs.

2. Meanwhile, in 12-inch skillet, melt butter over high heat. Add green onions, pepper, and ½ teaspoon salt and cook 2 minutes. Reduce heat to medium-high and cook until green onions are soft, 4 to 5 minutes longer. Stir in chicken broth; heat to boiling. Cover and keep warm.

3. In small bowl, mix yogurt, garlic, and ⅛ teaspoon salt until blended.

4. Drain pasta; return to saucepot. Add green-onion mixture; toss well. Serve yogurt mixture to spoon over each serving. Garnish with green onion tops.

EACH MAIN-DISH SERVING About 540 calories | 20 g protein | 96 g carbohydrate | 9 g total fat (2 g saturated) | 4 mg cholesterol | 735 mg sodium.

Vegetable Lasagna Toss

Beans are a great low-fat source of protein. Add broccoli and you'll get a healthy dose of fiber, too. Plus, the broccoli and tomatoes are loaded with vitamins and cancer-fighting phytochemicals. The Romano cheese provides full flavor (and calcium) without adding much fat.

PREP about 10 minutes   COOK about 20 minutes   MAKES 4 main-dish servings

8 ounces lasagna noodles

1 tablespoon extra virgin olive oil

2 cloves garlic, crushed with press

1 bag (12 ounces) broccoli florets

1 cup low-sodium chicken broth

1 can (15 to 19 ounces) white kidney beans (cannellini), drained and rinsed

3 large tomatoes, coarsely chopped

⅓ cup freshly grated Romano cheese, plus additional for serving

1. Heat 5- to 6-quart covered saucepot of salted water to boiling over high heat. Add noodles and cook until just tender, about 2 minutes longer than label directs.

2. Meanwhile, in nonstick 12-inch skillet, heat oil over medium heat; add garlic and broccoli and cook 1 minute, stirring frequently. Add broth; cover and cook 8 minutes. Stir in beans; cover and cook 2 to 3 minutes longer or until broccoli is very tender. Stir in tomatoes; remove from heat.

3. Drain lasagna noodles; add to broccoli mixture in skillet and sprinkle with Romano cheese. Toss to coat noodles. Serve with additional Romano if you like.

EACH SERVING 425 calories | 19 g protein | 71 g carbohydrate | 8 g total fat (2 g saturated) | 8 mg cholesterol | 380 mg sodium.

Pierogi with Caramelized Onion and Brussels Sprouts

These **Polish-style potato-cheese dumplings** make a quick, satisfying one-dish meal when teamed with **Brussels sprouts.** Look for pierogi in the freezer section of your supermarket.

PREP 20 minutes   **COOK** 30 minutes   **MAKES** 4 main-dish servings

2 tablespoons olive oil

1 jumbo onion (1 pound), cut in half and thinly sliced

2 teaspoons sugar

³/₄ teaspoon salt

2 containers (10 ounces each) Brussels sprouts, trimmed and thinly sliced

1 cup vegetable broth

¹/₄ teaspoon coarsely ground black pepper

1 package (16 to 19 ounces) frozen potato-and-Cheddar pierogi

¹/₄ cup walnuts, toasted (see Tip page 142) and chopped

1. In nonstick 12-inch skillet, heat oil over medium heat until hot. Add onion, sugar, and ¼ teaspoon salt, and cook 20 minutes or until onion is tender and caramelized, stirring occasionally.

2. Increase heat to medium-high; add Brussels sprouts, broth, black pepper, and remaining ½ teaspoon salt; cover and cook until the Brussels sprouts are tender, about 8 minutes, stirring occasionally.

3. Meanwhile, in large saucepot, cook pierogi as label directs.

4. Drain pierogi; toss with onion mixture and chopped walnuts.

EACH SERVING About 420 calories | 15 g protein | 63 g carbohydrate | 15 g total fat (3 g saturated) | 11 mg cholesterol | 1,205 mg sodium.

GH Test Kitchen Tip

Try to use Brussels sprouts within 2 or 3 days of purchase. If they are stored longer, their flavor becomes stronger.

Portobello Pasta

A delicious sauté of mushrooms, sweet red pepper, and onion tossed with bow-tie pasta and baby spinach.

PREP 10 minutes   COOK 20 minutes   MAKES 4 main-dish servings

1 tablespoon olive oil

1 large onion, cut in half and thinly sliced

1 large red pepper, thinly sliced

2 garlic cloves, crushed with garlic press

2 packages (6 ounces each) sliced Portobello mushrooms, each halved

1 tablespoon balsamic vinegar

1¼ teaspoons salt

¼ teaspoon ground black pepper

1 package (16 ounces) bow-tie pasta

1 bag (6 ounces) baby spinach

1. In nonstick 12-inch skillet, heat oil over medium heat until hot. Add onion and red pepper, and cook 10 to 12 minutes or until vegetables are tender and golden, stirring often. Add garlic and cook 30 seconds, stirring.

2. To onion mixture in skillet, add the mushrooms, vinegar, salt, and black pepper, and cook over medium-high heat about 10 minutes or until mushrooms are tender, stirring often.

3. Meanwhile, in large saucepot, cook pasta as label directs.

4. When pasta has cooked to desired doneness, remove *½ cup pasta cooking water* and reserve. Drain pasta. Return pasta to saucepot; stir in mushroom mixture, spinach, and reserved pasta cooking water.

EACH SERVING About 515 calories | 20 g protein | 96 carbohydrate | 5 g total fat (1 saturated) | 0 mg cholesterol | 1,000 mg sodium.

Penne with Yellow Peppers and Sweet Onion

Long, slow cooking makes sweet onion and yellow peppers even sweeter and more flavorful. Be sure to stir often to prevent scorching.

⏱ **PREP** 15 minutes **COOK** 15 minutes
MAKES 4 main-dish or 8 accompaniment servings

2 tablespoons olive oil

2 medium yellow peppers, thinly sliced

1 jumbo sweet onion (12 ounces) such as Walla Walla or Vidalia, thinly sliced

$\frac{1}{2}$ teaspoon salt

$\frac{1}{4}$ teaspoon coarsely ground black pepper

1 tablespoon balsamic vinegar

$\frac{1}{2}$ cup chopped fresh basil

1 package (16 ounces) penne rigate or elbow twist pasta

1. In 12-inch skillet heat olive oil over medium heat until hot. Add yellow peppers, onion, salt, and black pepper, and cook until vegetables are tender and golden, about 15 minutes, stirring frequently. Remove skillet from heat; stir in balsamic vinegar and chopped basil.

2. Meanwhile, in large saucepot, cook pasta as label directs.

3. When pasta has cooked to desired doneness, remove *½ cup pasta cooking water*. Drain pasta and return to saucepot. Add yellow-pepper mixture and reserved pasta cooking water; toss well.

EACH MAIN-DISH SERVING About 525 calories | 16 g protein | 95 g carbohydrate | 9 g total fat (1 g saturated) | 0 mg cholesterol | 455 mg sodium.

Linguine with Mushroom Sauce

This buttery sauce combines both dried and fresh mushrooms for rich, earthy flavor. Serve with a salad of baby greens tossed with a lemon vinaigrette.

PREP 20 minutes plus standing COOK 25 minutes MAKES 6 main-dish servings

½ cup boiling water

1 package (.35 ounce) dried porcini mushrooms

2 tablespoons olive oil

1 medium onion, chopped

2 garlic cloves, finely chopped

8 ounces shiitake mushrooms, stems removed and caps thinly sliced

12 ounces white mushrooms, trimmed and thinly sliced

½ teaspoon salt

¼ teaspoon freshly ground black pepper

1¼ cups chicken broth

1 package (16 ounces) linguine

2 tablespoons butter, cut into pieces (optional)

¼ cup chopped fresh parsley

1. In small bowl, pour boiling water over porcini mushrooms; let stand about 30 minutes. With slotted spoon, remove porcini. Rinse mushrooms to remove any grit, then chop. Strain mushroom liquid through sieve lined with paper towels; set aside.

2. In 12-inch skillet, heat 1 tablespoon oil over low heat. Add onion and garlic and cook, stirring frequently, until onion is tender. Add shiitake mushrooms and cook, stirring, 5 minutes. Add remaining 1 tablespoon oil, white and porcini mushrooms, salt, and pepper; cook until mushrooms are tender, about 7 minutes. Add reserved mushroom liquid and cook, stirring frequently, until liquid has evaporated, about 2 minutes. Add broth and heat to boiling; cook until broth has reduced by one-third.

3. Meanwhile, in large saucepot, cook pasta as label directs. Drain. In warm serving bowl, toss pasta with mushroom sauce, butter if using, and parsley.

EACH SERVING WITHOUT BUTTER About 366 calories | 13 g protein | 64 g carbohydrate | 6 g total fat (1 g saturated) | 0 mg cholesterol | 475 mg sodium.

Bow Ties with Swiss Chard and Pancetta

Chard has a mild, slightly beetlike flavor. Three types are generally available: green, golden, or red. Any will work well in this recipe.

PREP 25 minutes   **COOK** 35 minutes   **MAKES** 6 main-dish servings

2 large bunches Swiss chard (about 1¾ pounds each)

2 ounces pancetta, cut into ¼-inch dice

1 large onion, sliced

1 medium carrot, cut into ¼-inch dice

2 garlic cloves, minced

½ teaspoon salt

¼ teaspoon crushed red pepper

1 cup chicken broth

1 package (1 pound) bow-tie pasta

1. Trim off 2 inches from Swiss-chard stems; discard ends. Separate stems from leaves. Cut stems and leaves into ½-inch slices.

2. In deep nonstick 12-inch skillet, cook pancetta over medium-high heat 5 minutes or until golden, stirring frequently. With slotted spoon, transfer pancetta to small bowl.

3. To drippings remaining in skillet, add onion and carrot, and cook 10 minutes, stirring frequently. Add the Swiss-chard stems, garlic, salt, and red pepper, and cook 10 minutes or until tender and golden, stirring occasionally.

4. Gradually add Swiss-chard leaves, stirring, and cook until wilted and water evaporates, about 5 minutes. Add chicken broth and cook 1 minute.

5. Meanwhile, in large saucepot, cook pasta as label directs. Drain.

6. In large bowl, toss pasta with Swiss-chard mixture; sprinkle with pancetta.

EACH SERVING About 400 calories | 16 g protein | 70 g carbohydrate | 7 g total fat (2 g saturated) | 7 mg cholesterol | 870 mg sodium.

GH Test Kitchen Tip

Pancetta will keep for 3 weeks refrigerated or up to 6 months frozen.

Roasted Vegetables with Arugula and Whole-Wheat Fusilli

Sweet roasted squash, red peppers, and onions contrast nicely with peppery arugula. If you prefer, substitute regular pasta for the whole-wheat.

PREP 25 minutes   ROAST 50 minutes   MAKES 4 servings

1 package (about 20 ounces) butternut squash chunks, cut into 1-inch pieces

4 garlic cloves, each cut in half

2 medium red onions, each cut into 8 wedges

2 medium red peppers, cut into ½-inch-wide strips

2 tablespoons olive oil

¼ teaspoon coarsely ground black pepper

1 teaspoon salt

1 pound whole-wheat fusilli or corkscrew pasta

2 bunches arugula (about 4 ounces each),tough stems trimmed, leaves coarsely chopped

2 tablespoons white or dark balsamic vinegar

grated Parmesan cheese (optional)

1. Preheat oven to 450°F. Toss squash, garlic, onions, red peppers, oil, pepper, and salt in 15½" by 10½" jelly-roll pan until evenly mixed. Roast 50 minutes or until the vegetables are tender and lightly golden, stirring occasionally.

2. Meanwhile, in large saucepot, cook fusilli as label directs.

3. When pasta has cooked to desired doneness, remove ½ cup pasta cooking water; reserve. Drain pasta and return to saucepot. Add roasted vegetables, arugula, vinegar, and reserved pasta cooking water; toss until well mixed. Serve with Parmesan, if you like.

EACH SERVING About 610 calories | 19 g protein | 115 g carbohydrate | 9 g total fat (1 g saturated) | 0 mg cholesterol | 610 mg sodium.

Pasta Primavera

This dish is traditionally made in spring, when the first tender young vegetables appear—thus the name *primavera*, which means spring in Italian. We used fresh asparagus and sugar snaps and cooked them along with the pasta to save time (see photo on page 97).

PREP 15 minutes   COOK 25 minutes   MAKES 6 main-dish servings

$\frac{1}{2}$ cup heavy or whipping cream

3 tablespoons butter or margarine

4 ounces shiitake mushrooms, stems removed and caps thinly sliced

2 very small yellow squash or zucchini (4 ounces each), cut into 2" by $\frac{1}{4}$" matchstick strips

4 green onions, thinly sliced

1 tablespoon chopped fresh parsley

1 package (16 ounces) fettuccine

1 pound asparagus, trimmed and cut on diagonal into $1\frac{1}{2}$-inch pieces

4 ounces sugar snap peas, strings removed

$\frac{3}{4}$ cup freshly grated Parmesan cheese

$\frac{1}{4}$ teaspoon salt

1. In 1-quart saucepan, heat cream to boiling and boil 1 minute. Remove saucepan from heat and set aside.

2. In nonstick 10-inch skillet, melt butter or margarine over medium heat. Add mushrooms and cook, stirring, 1 minute. Add squash and cook, stirring, until vegetables are tender, about 3 minutes. Remove from heat; stir in green onions and parsley. Keep warm.

3. Meanwhile, in large saucepot, cook pasta as label directs. After pasta has cooked 7 minutes, add asparagus and sugar snap peas to pasta water. Cook until pasta and vegetables are tender, 3 to 5 minutes longer. Drain pasta and vegetables, reserving $\frac{1}{2}$ *cup pasta cooking water*.

4. In warm serving bowl, toss pasta and vegetables with reserved pasta water, Parmesan, and salt. Stir in cream and mushroom mixture.

EACH SERVING About 491 calories | 18 g protein | 64 g carbohydrate | 18 g total fat (11 g saturated) | 52 mg cholesterol | 462 mg sodium.

Vegetable Lo Mein

By using precut vegetables, we've eliminated much of the work in this Asian favorite. If you have access to an Asian market, substitute Chinese lo mein noodles for the linguine.

PREP 20 minutes   COOK 20 minutes   MAKES 4 main-dish servings

1 package (16 ounces) linguine or spaghetti

1/3 cup hoisin sauce

2 tablespoons reduced-sodium soy sauce

1/2 teaspoon cornstarch

3 teaspoons vegetable oil

1 package (10 ounces) sliced mushrooms

1 tablespoon grated, peeled fresh ginger

1 package (10 ounces) shredded carrots

3 small zucchini (about 6 ounces each), each cut lengthwise in half, then cut crosswise into 1/4-inch-thick slices

3 green onions, cut into 1-inch pieces

1 cup reduced-sodium chicken broth

2 tablespoons seasoned rice vinegar

1. In large saucepot, cook linguine as label directs but do not use salt.

2. Meanwhile, in cup, stir the hoisin sauce, soy sauce, and cornstarch until smooth; set aside.

3. In nonstick 12-inch skillet, heat 2 teaspoons vegetable oil over medium-high heat until hot. Add mushrooms and cook about 5 minutes or until mushrooms are golden and liquid evaporates, stirring frequently. Stir in ginger; cook 30 seconds. Remove mushroom mixture to bowl.

4. In same skillet, in remaining 1 teaspoon vegetable oil, cook carrots 2 minutes, stirring frequently. Stir in zucchini and green onions and cook about 10 minutes longer or until vegetables are tender-crisp. Stir in chicken

> ### GH Test Kitchen Tip
> Hoisin sauce, used in many Chinese dishes, is made from sugar, soybeans, sesame seeds, and spices and has a sweet/smoky taste. Once opened, it will keep in the refrigerator for several months.

broth, cornstarch mixture, and mushroom mixture. Heat to boiling; cook 1 minute.

5. To serve, toss linguine, vegetable mixture, and rice vinegar in large serving bowl.

EACH SERVING About 570 calories | 20 g protein | 111 g carbohydrate | 7 g total fat (1 g saturated) | 0 mg cholesterol | 970 mg sodium.

Sesame Noodles

Kids and grown-ups alike will take to this Chinese-restaurant favorite made with a peanut butter and sesame dressing spiked with orange juice.

PREP 15 minutes **COOK** 15 minutes **MAKES** 6 main-dish servings

1 package (16 ounces) spaghetti

1 cup fresh orange juice

$\frac{1}{4}$ cup seasoned rice vinegar

$\frac{1}{4}$ cup soy sauce

$\frac{1}{4}$ cup creamy peanut butter

1 tablespoon Asian sesame oil

1 tablespoon grated, peeled fresh ginger

2 teaspoons sugar

$\frac{1}{4}$ teaspoon crushed red pepper

1 bag (10 ounces) shredded carrots (about 3$\frac{1}{2}$ cups)

3 Kirby cucumbers (about 4 ounces each), unpeeled and cut into matchstick-thin strips

2 green onions, thinly sliced

2 tablespoons sesame seeds, toasted (optional)

green onions for garnish

1. In large saucepot, cook pasta as label directs.

2. Meanwhile, in medium bowl, with wire whisk or fork, mix orange juice, vinegar, soy sauce, peanut butter, oil, ginger, sugar, and crushed red pepper until blended; set the sauce aside.

3. Place carrots in colander; drain pasta over carrots. In large serving bowl, toss pasta mixture, cucumbers, and green onions with sauce. If you like, sprinkle the pasta with sesame seeds. Garnish with green onions.

EACH SERVING About 445 calories | 15 g protein | 76 g carbohydrate | 9 g total fat (2 g saturated) | 0 mg cholesterol | 1,135 mg sodium.

Classic Lasagna with Meat Sauce

Guys with big appetites—and just about everyone else—will love this hearty dish. We use both beef and Italian sausage to double the flavor and call for no-boil noodles to save time. If your package contains 15 noodles, use an extra noodle in each of the first 3 layers when assembling lasagna.

PREP 1 hour **BAKE** 30 minutes **MAKES** 10 main-dish servings

MEAT SAUCE

8 ounces sweet Italian-sausage links, casings removed

8 ounces lean ground beef

1 small onion, diced

2 garlic cloves, minced

1 can (28 ounces) plus 1 can (14½ to 16 ounces) whole tomatoes in juice

2 tablespoons tomato paste

½ teaspoon salt

2 tablespoons chopped fresh basil

CHEESE FILLING

1 large egg

¼ teaspoon coarsely ground black pepper

1 container (15 ounces) part-skim ricotta cheese

4 ounces part-skim mozzarella cheese, shredded (1 cup)

¾ cup grated Parmesan cheese

1 package (8 ounces) no-boil lasagna noodles (12 noodles)

1. Prepare meat sauce: Heat 4-quart saucepan over medium-high heat until hot. Add sausage and ground beef, and cook, stirring, 1 minute. Add onion and cook until meat is browned and onion is tender, about 5 minutes, stirring occasionally and breaking up sausage with side of spoon. Pour off drippings from saucepan. Add garlic to meat mixture in saucepan and cook 1 minute.

2. Stir in tomatoes with their juice, tomato paste, and salt, breaking up tomatoes with spoon; heat to boiling. Reduce heat to medium and cook, uncovered, 20 minutes, stirring occasionally. Stir in the basil. Makes about 6 cups sauce.

3. Prepare the cheese filling: In a medium bowl, mix egg, pepper, ricotta, ½ cup mozzarella, and ½ cup Parmesan until blended.

4. Preheat oven to 350°F. Into 13" by 9" glass baking dish, evenly spoon 2 cups sauce. Arrange 3 noodles over sauce, making sure noodles do not touch sides of dish (they will expand). Top with 1¼ cups ricotta mixture, 3 noodles, and 2 cups of sauce. Arrange 3 noodles on top; spread with remaining ricotta mixture. Top with remaining noodles and remaining sauce. Sprinkle with remaining ½ cup mozzarella and ¼ cup Parmesan. (If making a day ahead, cover and refrigerate.)

5. Cover lasagna with foil and bake 30 minutes (1 hour if refrigerated) or until hot and bubbly. Let lasagna stand 10 minutes for easier serving.

EACH SERVING About 350 calories | **24 g protein** | **27 g carbohydrate** | **16 g total fat (8 g saturated)** | **78 mg cholesterol** | **775 mg sodium.**

Vegetable Lasagna

So chock-full of vegetables and cheese, you'll never miss the meat. We recommend our homemade Marinara Sauce, but if you're in a rush, you can substitute an equal amount of jarred sauce.

PREP 1 hour BAKE 40 minutes MAKES 10 main-dish servings

Marinara Sauce (page 29)

12 lasagna noodles (10 ounces)

2 medium zucchini (8 ounces each), cut into ¼-inch-thick slices

2 tablespoons olive oil

¾ teaspoon salt

¼ teaspoon ground black pepper

1 garlic clove, finely chopped

⅛ teaspoon crushed red pepper

2 tablespoons all-purpose flour

⅔ cup milk, warmed

2 packages (10 ounces each) frozen chopped spinach, thawed and squeezed dry

2 tablespoons plus ¼ cup freshly grated Parmesan cheese

1 container (15 ounces) part-skim ricotta cheese

2 tablespoons chopped fresh parsley

4 ounces mozzarella cheese, shredded (1 cup)

1. Prepare marinara sauce.

2. Meanwhile, in large saucepot, cook lasagna noodles as label directs. Drain and rinse with cold running water. Return noodles to saucepot with enough cold water to cover.

3. Preheat oven to 450°F. In large bowl, toss zucchini with 1 tablespoon oil, ¼ teaspoon salt, and ⅛ teaspoon black pepper. Arrange zucchini slices on large cookie sheet and bake, turning once, until tender, about 12 minutes.

4. Meanwhile, in nonstick 12-inch skillet, heat remaining 1 tablespoon oil over medium heat. Add garlic and crushed red pepper; cook until garlic is golden. Stir in flour until blended. With wire whisk, gradually whisk in warm milk with wooden spoon. Cook, stirring constantly, until sauce has thickened and boils, about 2 minutes. Remove from heat and stir in spinach, 2 tablespoons Parmesan, and ¼ teaspoon salt.

5. In medium bowl, stir ricotta, parsley, remaining ¼ cup Parmesan, the remaining ¼ teaspoon salt, and the remaining ⅛ teaspoon black pepper until combined.

6. Turn oven control to 350°F. Drain lasagna noodles on clean kitchen towels.

7. In 13" by 9" baking dish, spread about 1 cup marinara sauce. Arrange 4 lasagna noodles over sauce, overlapping to fit. Spread ricotta mixture on top of noodles. Arrange 4 more noodles over ricotta and top with all of zucchini, overlapping slices to fit. Spread with 1 cup sauce and sprinkle with half of mozzarella; top with all of spinach mixture. Arrange remaining 4 noodles on top and spread with remaining marinara sauce. Sprinkle with remaining mozzarella.

8. Cover lasagna with foil and bake 30 minutes. Remove foil and bake until cheese is lightly golden, about 10 minutes longer. Let stand 15 minutes for easier serving.

EACH SERVING About 219 calories | 13 g protein | 14 g carbohydrate | 13 g total fat (5 g saturated) | 27 mg cholesterol | 687 mg sodium.

Tuscan Lasagna Spirals

Spinach, bacon, and Fontina cheese make a spectacular filling for lasagna. Both filling and sauce can be made a day ahead and refrigerated. Fill, roll, and bake as directed, but add about 15 minutes to the final baking time.

PREP 1 hour **BAKE** 55 minutes **MAKES** 6 main-dish servings

12 lasagna noodles

1 tablespoon olive oil

1 jumbo onion (about 1 pound), finely chopped

4 garlic cloves, crushed with garlic press

4 slices bacon (about 3 ounces), cut into ¼-inch pieces

1 pound white mushrooms, finely chopped

1 pound portobello mushrooms, stems removed and caps finely chopped

1 package (10 ounces) frozen chopped spinach, thawed and squeezed dry

4 ounces Fontina cheese, shredded (1 cup)

½ cup grated Parmesan cheese

½ teaspoon salt

¼ teaspoon coarsely ground black pepper

1 can (28 ounces) plus 1 can (14½ to 16 ounces) whole tomatoes in puree

⅓ cup water

1. In large saucepot, cook lasagna noodles as label directs. Drain noodles and rinse with cold running water; drain again. Layer noodles between sheets of waxed paper.

2. Preheat oven to 450°F. In nonstick 12-inch skillet, heat oil over medium heat until hot. Add onion and cook 12 to 15 minutes, until golden. Add garlic; cook 2 minutes longer, stirring frequently. Reserve ½ cup onion mixture for sauce; transfer remaining mixture to large bowl.

3. Add bacon to skillet and cook until browned, about 7 to 8 minutes, stirring occasionally. With slotted spoon, transfer bacon to bowl with onion mixture.

4. Into each of two 15½" by 10½" jelly-roll pans, spoon 2 teaspoons bacon fat from skillet. Discard any remaining fat; do not clean skillet. Place pans in oven; heat 3 minutes. Add white mushrooms to 1 pan; toss to coat. Add portobello mushrooms to other pan; toss to coat. Bake mushrooms, uncovered, 25 minutes or until lightly browned, rotating pans between upper and lower racks halfway through cooking time. Transfer all mushrooms to bowl with onion mixture; stir in spinach, Fontina, Parmesan, salt, and pepper. Turn oven control to 350°F.

5. In same skillet, heat both cans of tomatoes with their puree, water, and reserved onion mixture to boiling over medium-high heat, stirring occasionally and breaking up tomatoes with side of spoon. Reduce heat to low; cover and simmer sauce 10 minutes. Stir ½ cup sauce into mushroom mixture in bowl. Spoon remaining sauce into 13" by 9" glass baking dish.

6. On work surface, place 6 lasagna noodles. Spoon scant ½ cup mushroom filling down center of each noodle. Roll each noodle, jelly-roll fashion; place rolled noodles, filling side up, in dish with sauce. Repeat with remaining noodles and filling.

7. Cover and bake 30 minutes or until heated through.

EACH SERVING About 500 calories | 24 g protein | 66 g carbohydrate | 18 g total fat (8 g saturated) | 35 mg cholesterol | 1,360 mg sodium.

Butternut-Squash Lasagna

Celebrate autumn with this luscious roasted squash and chard main dish.

🖭 **PREP** I hour 15 minutes **BAKE** 40 minutes **MAKES** 10 main-dish servings

12 lasagna noodles

I large butternut squash (3 pounds),
  peeled, seeded, and cut into 1-
  inch chunks

2 tablespoons olive oil

¾ teaspoon salt

I jumbo onion (I pound), cut in half
  and thinly sliced

I large bunch Swiss chard (about
  1½ pounds), coarsely chopped,
  with tough stems discarded

WHITE SAUCE

2 tablespoons butter or margarine

⅓ cup all-purpose flour

¼ teaspoon coarsely ground
  black pepper

¼ teaspoon salt

¼ teaspoon ground nutmeg

¼ teaspoon dried thyme

4 cups low-fat (1%) milk

¾ cup grated Parmesan cheese

1. In saucepot, cook lasagna noodles as label directs. Drain noodles and rinse with cold running water; drain again. Layer noodles between sheets of waxed paper.

2. Meanwhile, preheat oven to 450°F. In large bowl, toss butternut squash chunks with 1 tablespoon olive oil and ½ teaspoon salt. Place squash on 15½" by 10½" jelly-roll pan or large cookie sheet. Roast squash 30 minutes or until fork-tender, stirring halfway through cooking. Remove from oven and, with fork or potato masher, mash squash until almost smooth; set aside. Turn oven control to 375°F.

3. Meanwhile, in 5-quart Dutch oven, heat remaining 1 tablespoon olive oil over medium heat until hot. Add onion and ¼ teaspoon salt, and cook about 25 minutes or until golden, stirring often. Add chard; cook until wilted and liquid evaporates, about 7 minutes. Remove Dutch oven from heat; set aside.

4. Prepare white sauce: In 3-quart saucepan, melt butter or margarine over medium heat. With wire whisk, stir in flour, pepper, salt, nutmeg, and thyme, and cook 1 minute, stirring constantly. Gradually whisk in milk and cook over medium-high heat, stirring frequently, until sauce boils and thickens slightly. Boil 1 minute, stirring. Whisk in all but 2 tablespoons Parmesan. Remove saucepan from heat.

5. In 13" by 9" glass baking dish, evenly spoon about ½ cup white sauce to cover bottom of dish. Arrange 4 lasagna noodles over sauce, overlapping to fit. Evenly spread all Swiss chard mixture over noodles and top with about 1 cup white sauce. Arrange 4 lasagna noodles on top, then about 1 cup white sauce and all butternut squash. Top with remaining lasagna noodles and remaining white sauce. Sprinkle with remaining 2 tablespoons Parmesan cheese.

6. Cover lasagna with foil and bake 30 minutes; remove foil and bake 10 minutes longer or until hot and bubbly. Let lasagna stand 10 minutes for easier serving.

EACH SERVING About 315 calories | 13 g protein | 47 g carbohydrate | 9 g total fat (3 g saturated) | 10 mg cholesterol | 575 mg sodium.

GH Test Kitchen Tip

Nutmeg is a natural in milk-based dishes. For best flavor, buy a whole nutmeg and grate it yourself just before using.

Capellini Frittata

Sautéed onion and red pepper flavor this light egg-and-pasta custard. If you have leftover spaghetti in the fridge, use 1 cup of it instead of the cooked capellini. Serve mango or melon wedges with a squeeze of lime for dessert.

PREP 14 minutes   **BAKE** 6 minutes   **MAKES** 4 main-dish servings

2 ounces capellini or angel hair pasta, broken into pieces (about ½ cup)

2 teaspoons olive oil

1 small onion, thinly sliced

1 small red pepper, diced

6 large egg whites

2 large eggs

⅓ cup grated Parmesan cheese

¼ cup fat-free (skim) milk

½ teaspoon salt

¼ teaspoon hot pepper sauce

1. In 2-quart saucepan, heat *3 cups water* to boiling over high heat. Add pasta and cook 2 minutes or just until tender. Drain the pasta and set aside.

2. Meanwhile, preheat oven to 425°F. In nonstick 10-inch skillet with oven-safe handle (or cover handle with heavy-duty foil for baking in oven later), heat olive oil over medium heat. Add onion and red pepper, and cook, stirring frequently, until vegetables are tender, about 7 minutes.

3. In large bowl, with wire whisk or fork, beat egg whites, whole eggs, Parmesan, milk, salt, and hot pepper sauce; stir in pasta. Pour egg mixture over onion mixture; cover and cook 3 minutes or until set around the edge. Uncover skillet and place in oven. Bake 6 minutes longer or until frittata is set in center.

4. To serve, invert frittata onto cutting board and cut into wedges.

EACH SERVING About 190 calories | 15 g protein | 15 g carbohydrate | 8 g total fat (3 g saturated) | 113 mg cholesterol | 545 mg sodium.

Family-Style Macaroni and Cheese

This new variation on an all-time favorite provides a stealthy way to get veggies past little mac-and-cheese fans. Instead of premixed vegetables, make up your own combination. You'll need about 1¾ cups. Good choices include peas, corn, lima beans, green beans, and chopped broccoli.

⌀ **PREP** 20 minutes **BAKE** 20 minutes **MAKES** 8 main-dish servings

1 package (16 ounces) fusilli or rotini pasta

2 tablespoons butter or margarine

3 tablespoons all-purpose flour

½ teaspoon salt

¼ teaspoon coarsely ground black pepper

pinch nutmeg

4 cups reduced-fat (2%) milk

1 package (8 ounces) pasteurized processed cheese spread, cut up

¼ cup grated Parmesan cheese

6 ounces extrasharp Cheddar cheese, shredded (1½ cups)

1 package (10 ounces) frozen mixed vegetables

1. In large saucepot, cook pasta as label directs. Preheat oven to 400°F.

2. Meanwhile, in 3-quart saucepan, melt butter over medium heat. With wire whisk, stir in flour, salt, pepper, and nutmeg; cook 1 minute, stirring constantly. Gradually whisk in milk and cook over medium-high heat, stirring constantly, until sauce boils and thickens slightly. Boil 1 minute. Stir in cheese spread, Parmesan, and 1 cup Cheddar just until cheeses melt. Remove saucepan from heat.

3. Place frozen vegetables in colander; drain pasta over vegetables. Return pasta mixture to saucepot. Stir in cheese sauce. Transfer pasta mixture to 13" by 9" glass baking dish. Sprinkle with remaining ½ cup Cheddar. Bake, uncovered, 20 minutes or until hot and bubbly and top is lightly browned.

EACH SERVING About 520 calories | 25 g protein | 58 g carbohydrate | 21 g total fat (12 g saturated) | 52 mg cholesterol | 845 mg sodium.

Macaroni and Cheese Deluxe

A great dish gets even better with the addition of blue cheese, crunchy toasted nuts, and Parmesan-dusted tomatoes. A great choice for casual entertaining.

PREP 30 minutes   **BAKE** 25 minutes   **MAKES** 6 main-dish servings

1 package (16 ounces) campanelle or penne pasta

3 tablespoons butter or margarine

1 medium onion, diced

2 tablespoons all-purpose flour

¼ teaspoon coarsely ground black pepper

¼ teaspoon ground red pepper (cayenne)

¼ teaspoon ground nutmeg

¼ teaspoon salt

4 cups low-fat (1%) milk

½ cup grated Parmesan cheese

1 cup frozen peas

4 ounces creamy blue cheese, such as Gorgonzola, cut up or crumbled into pieces

½ pint pear-shaped or round cherry tomatoes, each cut in half

½ cup walnuts, toasted (see Tip)

1. In large saucepot, cook pasta as label directs. Preheat oven to 400°F.

2. Meanwhile, in 3-quart saucepan, melt butter over medium heat; add onion and cook 8 to 10 minutes, until tender, stirring occasionally. With wire whisk, stir in flour, black pepper, ground red pepper, nutmeg, and salt, and cook 1 minute, stirring constantly. Gradually whisk in milk and cook over medium-high heat, stirring frequently, until sauce boils and thickens slightly. Boil 1 minute, stirring. Stir in ¼ cup Parmesan cheese. Remove the saucepan from heat.

3. Place frozen peas in colander; drain pasta over peas and return pasta mixture to saucepot. Stir in sauce and blue cheese. Transfer pasta mixture to deep 3-quart casserole.

GH Test Kitchen Tip

To toast walnuts, spread them in a single layer on a baking sheet, then bake in a 350°F oven, stirring occasionally, for about 10 minutes, or until fragrant.

---

4. In small bowl, toss tomato halves with remaining ¼ cup Parmesan cheese. Top casserole with tomato halves. Bake, uncovered, 20 minutes, or until hot and bubbly and top is lightly browned. Sprinkle with walnuts before serving.

EACH SERVING About 610 calories | 26 g protein | 76 g carbohydrate | 23 g total fat (6 g saturated) | 43 mg cholesterol | 965 mg sodium.

Reduced-Fat Macaroni and Cheese

So smooth and creamy no one would guess we've sneaked out 10 grams of fat per serving. It's old-fashioned goodness without the guilt.

PREP 20 minutes **BAKE/BROIL** 22 minutes
MAKES 8 accompaniment or 4 main-dish servings

8 ounces elbow macaroni twists

1 container (16 ounces) low-fat (1%) cottage cheese

2 tablespoons all-purpose flour

2 cups skim milk

4 ounces sharp Cheddar cheese, shredded (1 cup)

1 teaspoon salt

1/4 teaspoon ground black pepper

pinch ground nutmeg

1/4 cup freshly grated Parmesan cheese

1. Preheat oven to 375°F. Grease broiler-safe shallow 2½-quart casserole. In medium saucepot, cook macaroni as label directs, but do not add salt to water. Drain.

2. In food processor with knife blade attached, puree cottage cheese until smooth. (Or, in blender, puree cottage cheese with ¼ cup of milk in recipe until smooth.)

3. In 2-quart saucepan, blend flour with ¼ cup milk until smooth. With wire whisk, slowly stir in remaining milk until blended. Cook over medium heat, stirring, until mixture has thickened slightly and boils. Remove from heat; stir in cottage cheese, Cheddar, salt, pepper, and nutmeg.

4. Spoon macaroni into prepared casserole and cover with cheese sauce. Bake 20 minutes. Remove from oven; sprinkle with Parmesan. Turn oven control to broil.

5. Place casserole in broiler at closest position to heat source; broil until top is golden brown, 2 to 3 minutes.

EACH ACCOMPANIMENT SERVING About 251 calories | 18 g protein | 28 g carbohydrate | 7 g total fat (4 g saturated) | 21 mg cholesterol | 724 mg sodium.

Party Baked Rigatoni and Peas

With this easy make-ahead, the cook can enjoy the party. The pasta is baked in two dishes so one stays warm in the oven while guests help themselves to the other at the buffet table.

⏲ PREP 45 minutes BAKE 30 minutes MAKES 16 buffet or side-dish servings

8 tablespoons butter or margarine (1 stick)

½ cup all-purpose flour

7 cups milk, warmed

2 cups freshly grated Parmesan cheese

2 teaspoons salt

2 packages (16 ounces each) rigatoni or ziti

1 bag (20 ounces) frozen peas, thawed

2 cans (14½ ounces each) diced tomatoes

1 cup loosely packed fresh basil leaves, thinly sliced

½ cup plain dried bread crumbs

1. Prepare cheese sauce: In heavy 4-quart saucepan, melt 6 tablespoons butter over low heat. Add flour and cook, stirring, 2 minutes. With wire whisk, gradually whisk in warm milk. Cook over medium heat, stirring constantly with wooden spoon, until sauce has thickened and boils. Reduce heat and simmer, stirring frequently, about 5 minutes. Stir in 1½ cups Parmesan and salt. Remove from heat.

2. Meanwhile, in 12-quart saucepot, cook pasta as label directs; drain. Return rigatoni to saucepot.

3. Preheat oven to 350°F. Pour cheese sauce over rigatoni in saucepot, stirring to combine. Stir in peas, tomatoes with their juice, and basil. Spoon pasta mixture into two shallow 3½- to 4-quart casseroles or two 13" by 9" baking dishes.

4. In small saucepan, melt remaining 2 tablespoons butter or margarine over low heat. Remove from heat and stir in bread crumbs and remaining ½ cup Parmesan. Sprinkle topping over pasta. Bake until hot and bubbling and topping is golden, 30 to 35 minutes.

EACH SERVING About 450 calories | 19 g protein | 60 g carbohydrate | 15 g total fat (9 g saturated) | 41 mg cholesterol | 970 mg sodium.

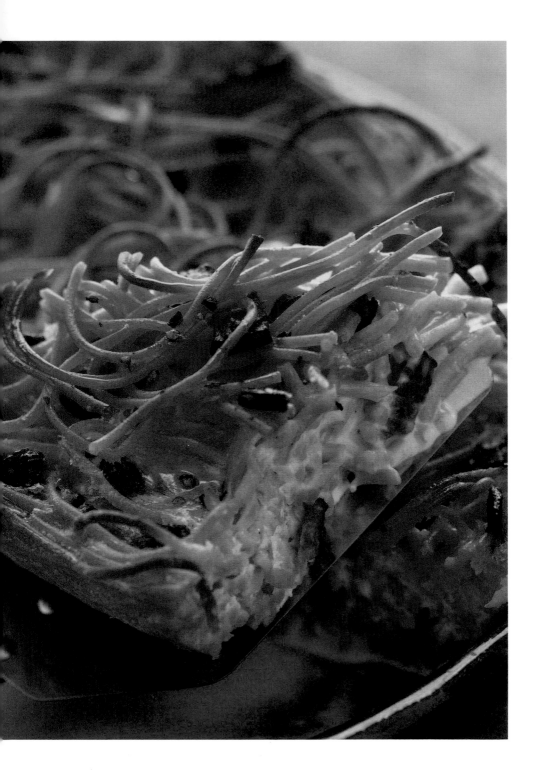

Spaghetti Carbonara Pie

Try this for brunch or on a chilly evening—it takes just minutes to prepare.

PREP 15 minutes   **BAKE** 35 to 40 minutes   **MAKES** 6 main-dish servings

12 ounces spaghetti

4 ounces bacon (about 6 slices), cut into 1/4-inch pieces

1 container (15 ounces) part-skim ricotta cheese

1/2 cup grated Pecorino Romano cheese

2 large eggs plus 1 large egg yolk

1/2 teaspoon coarsely ground black pepper

1/2 teaspoon salt

pinch nutmeg

2 cups milk

1. Preheat oven to 375°F. In large saucepot, cook spaghetti as label directs.

2. Meanwhile, in nonstick 10-inch skillet, cook the bacon over medium heat until browned, about 12 minutes. With slotted spoon, transfer bacon to paper towels to drain; set aside.

3. In blender at low speed, blend ricotta, Romano, eggs, egg yolk, pepper, salt, nutmeg, and 1/2 cup milk until smooth.

4. Drain pasta and return to saucepot. Add ricotta mixture, bacon, and remaining 1 1/2 cups milk, stirring to combine.

5. Transfer pasta mixture to 2 1/2-quart baking dish (about 2 inches deep). Bake 35 to 40 minutes, until golden around edges and almost set but still slightly liquid in center. Let pie stand 10 minutes before serving (liquid will be absorbed during standing). Cut into wedges to serve.

EACH SERVING About 470 calories | 25 g protein | 50 g carbohydrate | 18 g total fat (9 g saturated) | 154 mg cholesterol | 595 mg sodium.

Pasta e Fagioli Bake

We turned the much-loved Italian pasta-and-bean soup into a casserole by adding a little extra pasta, Romano cheese, and topping it with bread crumbs. Serve a tossed green salad on the side.

PREP 35 minutes   BAKE 15 minutes   MAKES 6 main-dish servings

8 ounces ditalini pasta (1¾ cups)

2 slices bacon, cut into ½-inch pieces

1 medium onion, diced

2 teaspoons plus 1 tablespoon olive oil

3 garlic cloves, minced

2 cans (15½ to 19 ounces each) white kidney beans (cannellini), rinsed and drained

1 can (16 ounces) plum tomatoes in juice

¾ cup chicken broth

¼ teaspoon coarsely ground black pepper

¼ cup plus 2 tablespoons grated Pecorino Romano cheese

2 slices firm white bread, torn into ¼-inch pieces

1 tablespoon chopped fresh parsley leaves

1. Preheat oven to 400°F. In large saucepot, cook pasta as label directs. Drain well, reserving *½ cup pasta cooking water.* Return the pasta to saucepot; set reserved cooking water aside.

2. Meanwhile, in 4-quart saucepan, cook bacon over medium heat until browned, stirring occasionally. Transfer bacon to paper towels to drain.

3. Pour off all but 1 teaspoon bacon fat from saucepan. Reduce heat to medium-low. Add onion and 2 teaspoons olive oil, and cook 5 minutes or until onion is tender, stirring occasionally. Stir in 1 teaspoon minced garlic, and cook 1 minute, stirring. Stir in beans, tomatoes with their juice, chicken broth, pepper, and cooked bacon, breaking up tomatoes with side of spoon; heat to boiling over high heat. Reduce heat to medium and simmer mixture, uncovered, 5 minutes, stirring occasionally.

4. To pasta in saucepot, add bean mixture, ¼ cup Romano cheese, and reserved pasta cooking water; toss well. Transfer mixture to 3-quart casserole.

5. In small bowl, toss bread crumbs with parsley, remaining olive oil, remaining minced garlic, and remaining 2 tablespoons Romano cheese until evenly coated. Sprinkle crumb mixture over pasta. Bake pasta 15 minutes, uncovered, until hot and bubbly and top is golden.

EACH SERVING About 405 calories | 19 g protein | 63 g carbohydrate | 9 g total fat (3 g saturated) | 9 mg cholesterol | 815 mg sodium.

Ziti with Eggplant and Ricotta

Make everyone feel special by serving this in individual gratin dishes, hot and bubbly from the oven. The sauce and eggplant can be prepared ahead and refrigerated separately. Cook pasta and assemble and bake as directed, adding about 10 minutes to the baking time to compensate for the chilled ingredients.

PREP 40 minutes   BAKE 20 minutes   MAKES 6 main-dish servings

1 medium eggplant (about 1½ pounds), cut into 1-inch pieces

3 tablespoons olive oil

¾ teaspoon salt

1 small onion, finely chopped

2 garlic cloves, minced

1 can (28 ounces) plum tomatoes in juice

2 tablespoons tomato paste

¼ teaspoon coarsely ground black pepper

3 tablespoons chopped fresh basil leaves

1 package (16 ounces) ziti or penne pasta

¼ cup grated Parmesan cheese

1 cup ricotta cheese

1. Preheat oven to 450°F. In large bowl, toss eggplant, 2 tablespoons olive oil, and ¼ teaspoon salt until evenly coated. Arrange eggplant in single layer in two 15½" by 10½" jelly-roll pans or 2 large cookie sheets. Place pans with eggplant on 2 oven racks in oven. Roast eggplant 30 minutes, rotating pans between upper and lower racks halfway through cooking and stirring twice, or until eggplant is tender and golden. Remove pans with eggplant from oven; set aside. Turn oven control to 400°F.

2. Meanwhile, in 3-quart saucepan, heat remaining 1 tablespoon olive oil over medium heat until hot. Add onion and cook until tender, about 5 minutes, stirring occasionally. Add garlic and cook 1 minute longer, stirring frequently.

3. Stir in tomatoes with their juice, tomato paste, pepper, and ½ teaspoon salt, breaking up tomatoes with side of spoon; heat to boiling over high heat. Reduce heat to low and simmer, uncovered, 10 minutes or until sauce thickens slightly. Stir in 2 tablespoons chopped fresh basil.

4. In large saucepot, cook pasta as label directs. Drain; return pasta to saucepot.

5. To pasta in saucepot, add roasted eggplant, tomato sauce, and Parmesan cheese; toss until evenly mixed. Spoon mixture into six 2-cup gratin dishes or shallow casseroles; top with dollops of ricotta cheese.

6. Cover casseroles with foil and bake 20 minutes or until hot and bubbly. To serve, sprinkle tops with remaining 1 tablespoon chopped fresh basil.

EACH SERVING About 500 calories | 19 g protein | 73 g carbohydrate | 15 g total fat (5 g saturated) | 24 mg cholesterol | 695 mg sodium.

Sunday Baked Ziti and Meatball Casserole

A crowd pleaser that's easy to prepare. If you're in a time crunch, use four cups of your favorite jarred tomato sauce (see photo on page 131).

PREP 30 minutes   BAKE 25 minutes   MAKES 8 main-dish servings

1 package (16 ounces) ziti or penne pasta

4 cups Big-Batch Tomato Sauce (page 33)

1 large egg

1 container (15 ounces) part-skim ricotta cheese

2 tablespoons grated Parmesan cheese

1 tablespoon chopped fresh parsley

1/2 teaspoon salt

1/4 teaspoon coarsely ground black pepper

8 frozen Lean Meatballs (page 39), thawed (see Tip) and sliced

1 package (4 ounces) shredded part-skim mozzarella cheese (1 cup)

1. In saucepot, cook pasta as label directs; drain. Return pasta to saucepot.

2. Meanwhile, in 3-quart saucepan, heat tomato sauce, covered, until hot over medium-low heat. (If tomato sauce is frozen, add *2 tablespoons water* to saucepan to prevent scorching.) Add 3 cups sauce to the pasta in the saucepot; toss well. Reserve remaining 1 cup sauce.

3. In medium bowl, stir together egg, ricotta cheese, Parmesan cheese, parsley, salt, and pepper.

4. Preheat oven to 400°F. Into 3½- to 4-quart shallow casserole or 13" by 9" glass baking dish, spoon half the pasta mixture; top with all the sliced meatballs. Drop ricotta-cheese mixture by spoonfuls evenly over meatball layer. Spoon remaining pasta mixture over ricotta-cheese layer, then spoon remaining 1 cup sauce over pasta. Sprinkle with shredded mozzarella cheese.

5. Bake, uncovered, 25 minutes or until very hot and cheese browns slightly.

EACH SERVING About 470 calories | 29 g protein | 55 g carbohydrate | 13 g total fat (5 g saturated) | 79 mg cholesterol | 1,040 mg sodium.

Photography Credits

Index

Metric Conversion Chart

The recipes that appear in this cookbook use the standard United States method for measuring liquid and dry or solid ingredients (teaspoons, tablespoons, and cups). The information on this chart is provided to help cooks outside the U.S. successfully use these recipes. All equivalents are approximate.

METRIC EQUIVALENTS FOR DIFFERENT TYPES OF INGREDIENTS

A standard cup measure of a dry or solid ingredient will vary in weight depending on the type of ingredient. A standard cup of liquid is the same volume for any type of liquid. Use the following chart when converting standard cup measures to grams (weight) or milliliters (volume).

Standard Cup	Fine Powder (e.g., flour)	Grain (e.g., rice)	Granular (e.g., sugar)	Liquid Solids (e.g., butter)	Liquid (e.g., milk)
1	140 g	150 g	190 g	200 g	240 ml
3/4	105 g	113 g	143 g	150 g	180 ml
2/3	93 g	100 g	125 g	133 g	160 ml
1/2	70 g	75 g	95 g	100 g	120 ml
1/3	47 g	50 g	63 g	67 g	80 ml
1/4	35 g	38 g	48 g	50 g	60 ml
1/8	18 g	19 g	24 g	25 g	30 ml

USEFUL EQUIVALENTS FOR LIQUID INGREDIENTS BY VOLUME

1/4 tsp	=				1 ml
1/2 tsp	=				2 ml
1 tsp	=				5 ml
3 tsp	= 1 tbls	=	1/2 fl oz	=	15 ml
	2 tbls	= 1/8 cup	= 1 fl oz	=	30 ml
	4 tbls	= 1/4 cup	= 2 fl oz	=	60 ml
	5 1/3 tbls	= 1/3 cup	= 3 fl oz	=	80 ml
	8 tbls	= 1/2 cup	= 4 fl oz	=	120 ml
	10 2/3 tbls	= 2/3 cup	= 5 fl oz	=	160 ml
	12 tbls	= 3/4 cup	= 6 fl oz	=	180 ml
	16 tbls	= 1 cup	= 8 fl oz	=	240 ml
	1 pt	= 2 cups	= 16 fl oz	=	480 ml
	1 qt	= 4 cups	= 32 fl oz	=	960 ml
			33 fl oz	=	1000 ml = 1 l

USEFUL EQUIVALENTS FOR DRY INGREDIENTS BY WEIGHT

(To convert ounces to grams, multiply the number of ounces by 30.)

1 oz	=	1/16 lb	=	30 g
4 oz	=	1/4 lb	=	120 g
8 oz	=	1/2 lb	=	240 g
12 oz	=	3/4 lb	=	360 g
16 oz	=	1 lb	=	480 g

USEFUL EQUIVALENTS FOR COOKING/OVEN TEMPERATURES

	Fahrenheit	Celsius	Gas Mark
Freeze Water	32° F	0° C	
Room Temperature	68° F	20° C	
Boil Water	212° F	100° C	
Bake	325° F	160° C	3
	350° F	180° C	4
	375° F	190° C	5
	400° F	200° C	6
	425° F	220° C	7
	450° F	230° C	8
Broil			Grill

USEFUL EQUIVALENTS FOR LENGTH

(To convert inches to centimeters, multiply the number of inches by 2.5.)

1 in	=		2.5 cm
6 in	= 1/2 ft	=	15 cm
12 in	= 1 ft	=	30 cm
36 in	= 3 ft	= 1 yd	= 90 cm
40 in	=		100 cm = 1 m

Rosemary Ellis — Editor in Chief

Susan Westmoreland — Food Director

Susan Deborah Goldsmith — Associate Food Director

Delia Hammock — Nutrition Director

Sharon Franke — Food Appliances Director

Richard Eisenberg — Special Projects Director

Supplemental Text by Anne Wright
Book design by Richard Oriolo

The first edition of this book was
cataloged by the Library of Congress
as follows:
Good Housekeeping 100 best pasta
recipes.
    p. cm.
  ISBN 1-58816-671-6
  1. Cookery (Pasta) I. Good
Housekeeping Institute (New York,
N.Y.)
  TX809.M17G65 2003
  641.8'22--dc21
                        2003000175

10 9 8 7 6 5 4 3 2 1

Published by Hearst Books
A Division of Sterling Publishing
Company, Inc.
387 Park Avenue South,
New York, NY 10016

Good Housekeeping and Hearst Books
are trademarks of Hearst
Communications, Inc.

The Good Housekeeping Cookbook
Seal guarantees that the recipes in this
cookbook meet the strict standards of
the Good Housekeeping Research
Institute, a source of reliable information
and a consumer advocate since 1900.
Every recipe has been triple-tested for
ease, reliability, and great taste.

www.goodhousekeeping.com

Distributed in Canada by
Sterling Publishing
℅ Canadian Manda Group,
165 Dufferin Street
Toronto, Ontario, Canada M6K 3H6

Distributed in Australia by Capricorn
Link (Australia) Pty. Ltd.
P.O. Box 704, Windsor, NSW 2756
Australia

Manufactured in China

Sterling ISBN-13: 978-1-58816-671-5
ISBN-10: 1-58816-671-6